To
Richard Bauckham
and
Larry Hurtado,
partners in dialogue

DID THE FIRST CHRISTIANS WORSHIP JESUS?

The New Testament evidence

JAMES D. G. DUNN

SPCK

WJK WESTMINSTER
JOHN KNOX PRESS
LOUISVILLE · KENTUCKY

First published in Great Britain in 2010 by
Society for Promoting Christian Knowledge
36 Causton Street
London SW1P 4ST

Published in 2010 in the United States of America by
Westminster John Knox Press
100 Witherspoon Street
Louisville, KY 40202

10 11 12 13 14 15 16 17 18 19 — 10 9 8 7 6 5 4 3 2 1

British Library Cataloguing-in-Publication Data
A catalogue record for this book is available from the British Library

ISBN 978-0-281-05928-7 (U.K. edition)

United States Library of Congress Cataloging-in-Publication Data
Dunn, James D. G., 1939–
Did the first Christians worship Jesus? : the New Testament evidence / James D. G. Dunn.
p. cm.
Includes bibliographical references (p. 152) and indexes.
ISBN 978-0-664-23196-5 (alk. paper)
1. Jesus Christ—Cult—History. 2. Worship in the Bible. 3. Jesus Christ—Divinity—
History of doctrines—Early church, ca. 30–600. 4. Bible. N.T.—Theology. I. Title.
BT590.C85D86 2010
232'.809015—dc22
2009049234

Typeset by Graphicraft Limited, Hong Kong
Printed in Great Britain by MPG

Produced on paper from sustainable forests

Contents

Contents

Abbreviations

ABD	D. N. Freedman (ed.), *Anchor Bible Dictionary* (6 vols; New York: Doubleday, 1992)
ALD	C. T. Lewis, *A Latin Dictionary* (Oxford: Clarendon, 1879)
BDAG	W. Bauer, *A Greek–English Lexicon of the New Testament and Other Early Christian Literature*, ET W. F. Arndt and F. W. Gingrich (eds), 3rd edition revised by F. W. Danker (Chicago: University of Chicago Press, 2000)
BCE	Before the Christian Era, or, Before the Common Era
BZNW	*Beihefte zur Zeitschrift für die neutestamentliche Wissenschaft*
CE	Christian Era, or, Common Era
EKK	Evangelisch-katholischer Kommentar zum Neuen Testament
ET	English translation
FS	Festschrift, volume written in honour of
HNT	Handbuch zum Neuen Testament
HUCA	*Hebrew Union College Annual*
ICC	International Critical Commentary
JJS	*Journal of Jewish Studies*
JQR	*Jewish Quarterly Review*
JR	*Journal of Religion*
*JSJ*Supp	*Journal for the Study of Judaism* Supplement Series
JSNT	*Journal for the Study of the New Testament*
JSNTS	*JSNT* Supplement Series
JSOT	Journal for the Study of the Old Testament
JTS	*Journal of Theological Studies*
LCL	Loeb Classical Library
LXX	Septuagint

MT	Masoretic Text
NIGTC	New International Greek Testament Commentary
NIV	New International Version (1978)
NJB	New Jerusalem Bible (1985)
NovT	*Novum Testamentum*
NRSV	New Revised Standard Version (1989)
NT	New Testament
NTS	*New Testament Studies*
*OCD*³	S. Hornblower and A. Spawforth (eds), *The Oxford Classical Dictionary* (3rd edition; Oxford: Clarendon Press, 2003)
ODCC	F. L. Cross and E. A. Livingstone (eds), *The Oxford Dictionary of the Christian Church* (2nd edition; Oxford: Oxford University Press, 1983)
OT	Old Testament
OTP	J. H. Charlesworth (ed.), *The Old Testament Pseudepigrapha* (2 vols; London: Darton, Longman & Todd, 1983, 1985)
REB	Revised English Bible (1989)
SNTSMS	Society for New Testament Studies Monograph Series
TDNT	G. Kittel and G. Friedrich (eds), *Theological Dictionary of the New Testament* (ET; Grand Rapids: Eerdmans, 1964–76)
TDOT	G. J. Botterweck and H. Ringgren (eds), *Theological Dictionary of the Old Testament* (ET; Grand Rapids: Eerdmans, 1974–2006)
WBC	Word Biblical Commentary
WUNT	Wissenschaftliche Untersuchungen zum Neuen Testament

Introduction

The question

The status accorded to or recognized for Jesus is the key distinctive and defining feature of Christianity. It is also the chief stumbling block for inter-faith dialogue between Christians and Jews, and between Christians and Muslims. Jew and Muslim simply cannot accept the divine status of Jesus as the Son of God, which Christians regard as fundamental to their faith. The Christian understanding of God as Trinity baffles them. To regard Jesus as divine, as worthy of worship as God, seems to them an obvious rejection of the oneness of God, more a form of polytheism than a form of monotheism. And truth to tell, many Christians also find the understanding of God as Trinity baffling. The confession of the Trinity in terms of 'essence' (or 'substance') makes too little sense, apart from the Greek philosophical categories that the language presupposes, for it to be very meaningful for most of those who repeat the Nicene Creed. And the classic creedal distinction between different 'persons' of the Godhead, when 'person' is understood in its everyday sense, invites the perception of God in tritheistic rather than Trinitarian terms, as three and distinct individual 'persons'.[1]

In view of this, it may be helpful to look back to the beginning of the process that resulted in the formulation of the Christian doctrine of the Trinity, and in doing so to clarify what lay behind the confession of Jesus as the Son of God in Trinitarian terms. The language of 'essence'/'substance' and 'person' was, of course, carefully chosen and the usage of these

---

[1] The problem was highlighted by both K. Rahner, *The Trinity* (London: Burns & Oates, 1970) 48, and G. W. H. Lampe, *God as Spirit* (Oxford University Press, 1977) 227–8.

terms was finely tuned by the controversies over the precise status of Jesus that racked the first few centuries of Christianity. But most Christians and most inter-faith dialogue would find it hard to recover and to appreciate that fine-tuning without an intensity of immersion in ancient philosophical debates that few could contemplate or have time for. Perhaps, then, a more fruitful way forward would be to inquire behind the process that has given Christianity its creedal confessions, to attempt some closer examination of the beginning of the process – what it was that launched the process, what it was that made Christians want to speak of Jesus in divine terms, what it was that led to the worship of Jesus as God.

The title of this book is of course controversial – intentionally so, because the issue itself is unavoidably controversial – *Did the First Christians Worship Jesus?* The immediate answer that most Christians will want to give is, 'Of course they did.' And if they want to cite some evidence by way of proof, they may well turn immediately to one of the closing scenes of John's Gospel, where Thomas, one of Jesus' twelve close disciples, addresses the resurrected Jesus as 'My Lord and my God' (John 20.28) – that is in terms of confessional worship. Or they could cite Paul's great poem/hymn in his letter to the Philippians, which climaxes in every knee in heaven and earth bowing and every tongue confessing that Jesus Christ is Lord (Phil. 2.10–11). Or they could refer to the book of Revelation, where the seer envisions myriads of myriads singing with full voice, 'Worthy is the Lamb that was slaughtered to receive power and wealth and wisdom and might and honour and glory and blessing' (Rev. 5.11–12). Of course the first Christians worshipped Jesus.

At the same time, however, the element of controversy cannot be excluded or ignored. For the New Testament also includes accounts of Jesus himself rebuking the thought that anyone might be worshipped other than God. When, in the story of Jesus' temptations, Satan invites Jesus to worship him, Jesus replies explicitly, 'Worship the Lord your God, and serve only him' (Matt. 4.10/Luke 4.8). The question unavoidably arises, 'Would Jesus have similarly rebuked those who sought to worship him?' Elsewhere, Jesus is recalled as maintaining the unique otherness that is God's alone. For example, when addressed by one seeking eternal life as 'Good teacher', Jesus replies, 'Why do you call me good? No one is good but God alone' (Mark 10.17–18). Again an unavoidable question arises: 'Would Jesus himself have welcomed his being confessed as equal with God?' Or take one other example, this time from Paul: a noticeable feature in his letters is his regular reference to Jesus as Lord, where, as we shall see, the title most obviously avers a divine status for Jesus; yet in several passages Paul also speaks of God as 'the God . . . of our Lord Jesus Christ'.[2] God is *the God of Jesus*, even of Jesus as *Lord*.

Of course, both aspects of the New Testament evidence need to be examined more closely. And there is much else, even within the first generation or two of Christianity, that calls for attention if we are to answer even such an apparently straightforward question as 'Did the first Christians worship Jesus?' But it is well that we begin with the realization that to answer the question effectively will require more than the citing of a few texts. We should also recognize that the way to the answer may be more difficult or challenging than at first appeared, and that the answer to the question may be less straightforward than we might like.

Those familiar with recent discussion in this area will be well aware of the considerable contribution to that discussion made by two senior scholars in Britain. Larry Hurtado (Edinburgh) has provided a series of studies developing the central claim that cultic devotion to Jesus was practised within a few years of Christianity's beginnings (that is not as a late development in early Christianity), and within an exclusivist commitment to the one God of the Bible.[3] During the same period Richard

---

[2] Rom. 15.6; 2 Cor. 1.3; 11.31; Col. 1.3; Eph. 1.3, 17; also 1 Pet. 1.3.
[3] Particularly L. W. Hurtado, *Lord Jesus Christ: Devotion to Jesus in Earliest Christianity* (Grand Rapids: Eerdmans, 2003); also *At the Origins of Christian Worship: The Context and Character of Earliest Christian Devotion* (Grand Rapids: Eerdmans, 1999); also *How on Earth Did Jesus Become a God? Historical Questions about Earliest Devotion to Jesus* (Grand Rapids: Eerdmans, 2005). Hurtado's stated aim is 'to

Bauckham (formerly of St Andrews) has been developing an impressive argument that Jesus was worshipped more or less from the beginning of Palestinian Jewish Christianity as one who shared or was included in the unique identity of the one God of Israel ('christological monotheism').[4] It is the emphasis that both Hurtado and Bauckham place on the worship of (or cultic devotion to) Jesus in earliest Christianity, and the import- ance they attribute to the actual practice and experience of this worship in shaping and determining the christology of the first Christians, that has suggested to me that a focused study on this central question ('Did the first Christians worship Jesus?') is desirable. I make bold to enter the discussion, not because I particularly disagree with Hurtado and Bauckham – our agreement on the great majority of the texts and issues discussed is substantial – but rather because I am concerned to ensure that the *whole* picture is brought into view, and that texts that indicate a greater complexity, and may even jar with the principal texts that have shaped Hurtado's and Bauckham's views, are not neglected. For if the full range of material points to answers like 'Yes, but to be noted also . . .', rather than a simple 'Yes' to our central question, then it is important that

---

demonstrate that Christ was given the sorts of devotion that we can properly understand as full cultic worship, and that we can rightly describe Christian worship of the earliest observable decades as genuinely "binitarian". That is, I contend that at this surprisingly early stage Christian worship has two recipients, God and Christ, yet the early Christians understand themselves as monotheists and see their inclu- sion of Christ in their devotional life as in no way compromising the uniqueness of the one God to whom they had been converted through the gospel' (*Origins* 5; see also 95–7; *Lord Jesus Christ* 50–3, 134–53; *How on Earth* 48–53).

[4] Particularly R. Bauckham, *Jesus and the God of Israel* (Milton Keynes: Paternoster, 2008), which includes several essay-length studies on the NT's christology of 'divine identity', and especially his *God Crucified: Monotheism and Christology in the New Testament* (Carlisle: Paternoster, 1998). The thesis is clearly stated in the opening pages of *God Crucified* (vii–viii) and of *Jesus and the God of Israel* (ix–x). He begins his revised article on 'Jesus, Worship of', from *ABD* 3.812–19: 'The prevalence and centrality of the worship of Jesus in early Christianity from an early date has frequently been underestimated, as has its importance for understanding christo- logical development' (*Jesus and the God of Israel* 127).

4

such material is not sidelined or ignored.[5] The desire to find an elegant summary or straightforward narrative in dealing with such profundities is natural and understandable. But it may be that the truth of God (including 'christological monotheism') eludes such neatness of expression. If so, it is as well that we are open to that possibility. Otherwise we may run the risk of thinking that we have actually succeeded in expressing adequately the inexpressible.[6]

The scope of our inquiry is very limited – limited mainly to the first generation of Christianity (including, unavoidably, Paul in particular), but with the recognition that we cannot hope to exclude the rest of the New Testament. Even that will be challenging enough, particularly as we try to hear how these

---

[5] In *Origins* 90–2 Hurtado responds to my earlier attempts to do justice to the full range of relevant material in Paul in *The Theology of Paul the Apostle* (Grand Rapids: Eerdmans/Edinburgh: T&T Clark, 1998) 257–60, where I suggest that Paul showed a degree of 'reserve' in relation to worship of Jesus and that we need 'a more carefully nuanced formulation in speaking about the cultic veneration of Jesus in earliest Christianity' (260). In contrast Hurtado maintains that 'there is no indication in Paul's letters that among the problems he had to deal with was anxiety about devotion to Jesus representing a possible neglect of God or threat to God's centrality' (*Origins* 91–2). In fact I do not disagree with that, and 'reserve' may not have been the best word to summarize the brief documentation of Pauline language and usage provided in *Theology* at that point. But it still seems to me to be relevant and potentially important to ask whether the first Christians used the full language and practice of worship in their devotion to Jesus, and, if not, to ask what stopped or inhibited them from doing so, and thence to explore the significance of the full range of NT data on the subject.

[6] The debate on the exegesis and issues involved has become quite intense and I will include others in the discussion, particularly W. Horbury, *Jewish Messianism and the Cult of Christ* (London: SCM Press, 1998); C. C. Newman, J. A. Davila and G. S. Lewis (eds), *The Jewish Roots of Christological Monotheism* (*JSJ*Supp 63; Leiden: Brill, 1999); L. T. Stuckenbruck and W. E. S. North (eds), *Early Jewish and Christian Monotheism* (JSNTS 263; London: T&T Clark, 2004); G. D. Fee, *Pauline Christology: An Exegetical–Theological Study* (Peabody: Hendrickson, 2007); and J. F. McGrath, *The Only True God: Early Christian Monotheism in its Jewish Context* (Champaign: University of Illinois Press, 2009). I have already responded to P. M. Casey, *From Jewish Prophet to Gentile God: The Origins and Development of New Testament Christology* (Cambridge: James Clarke, 1991) in 'The Making of Christology – Evolution or Unfolding?', in J. B. Green and M. Turner (eds), *Jesus of Nazareth, Lord and Christ*; I. H. Marshall FS (Grand Rapids: Eerdmans, 1994) 437–52.

texts were heard (and intended to be heard) by their first recipients, without that initial voice being drowned out by the way the same texts often came to be heard in the controversies of the second to fourth centuries.

The way forward will be as follows:

1 We need to consider whether 'worship' was given only to God (or gods). We must attempt to define what worship is and whether it is the fact that worship is offered to God (or a god) that in effect defines him (or her) as 'God'/'god'.

2 We need to ask what the worship of the God of Israel involved. What did it mean to 'worship the Lord God and serve only him'?

3 Since worship is the human response to what is perceived as God's self-revelation, we will look at how that self-revelation was perceived within Israel and in the religion within which Jesus and the first Christians (all Jews) grew up.

4 We will address the question of whether Jesus was a monotheist. Did he affirm the oneness of God as his ancestral faith insisted?

5 We will examine the conviction that God had exalted Jesus to his right hand, and how that contributed to Christian recognition of the divine status of Jesus. What did that mean for the first Christians? Did it involve a reassessment and restatement of the character of God as well as a re-appreciation of the status of Jesus?

What I hope will become apparent is that the first Christians did not see worship of Jesus as an alternative to worship of God. Rather, it was a way of worshipping God. That is to say, worship of Jesus is only possible or acceptable within what is now understood to be a Trinitarian framework. Worship of Jesus that is not worship of God through Jesus, or, more completely, worship of God through Jesus and in the Spirit, is not Christian worship.

1

The language of worship

What does the word 'worship' mean? What does the use of the word say about the one 'worshipped'? The question arises immediately for us since we are concerned with the worship of Jesus. If the first Christians did 'worship' Jesus what does that tell us about the status that they accorded to him? One way of defining 'worship' would be to confine its application to deity – worship as religious devotion paid to a god, or in the words of *The Concise Oxford Dictionary*, as 'reverence paid to God or god'. To 'worship' someone or some being would be to affirm their deity, to recognize that the someone or some being is God or a god. The problem, however, is that the term 'worship' is also used more widely. In the British legal system judges have regularly been addressed as 'Your Worship'. In the marriage service in the Book of Common Prayer the words are to be used, 'With my body I thee worship'. Everyday speech uses phrases like 'hero worship'. In these cases the language of course signals respect for someone regarded as of higher status and/or worthy of such respect. But such language does not indicate the deity of the one being thus 'worshipped'.

So we must reflect on the language of worship to help clarify what our central question means, or what its use in relation to Jesus expresses of Jesus' status or of the worshippers' regard for him. Both Hurtado and Bauckham marshal a good deal of the evidence regarding the language of worship used in relation to Jesus. But a more extensive and detailed study of the range of meaning of the word(s) usually translated as 'worship' in the New Testament seems to be called for, and this should help us to define what the first Christians understood by 'worship' more accurately and more fully.

We also need to take account of the range of near synonyms or alternatives to 'worship' – reverence, venerate, praise, glorify, adore, express devotion to, and so on. Here we run into a similar quandary. For just as a judge may be addressed as 'Your Worship', so in the history of Christianity, members of the clergy have often been addressed as 'Your reverence'. So too in the Church of England archdeacons have the title 'Venerable', and in Roman Catholic tradition 'venerable' is used of those whose sanctity is thereby recognized but who have still to be canonized, or recognized as 'saints'. We must also take note of the earlier debates within Christianity as to whether certain of these near synonyms or alternatives to 'worship' could be used in reference to the saints or the Virgin Mary. The clarification required to answer our question satisfactorily would seem to be more extensive than was first apparent.

1.1 To worship

The word most often translated as 'worship' in the New Testament is the Greek term *proskynein*. In turn, in the Septuagint (the Greek translation of the Hebrew Bible/Old Testament) *proskynein* is the regular translation of the Hebrew *shachah*. *Shachah* in the Hebrew Bible has the basic meaning of 'bow down, prostrate oneself, make obeisance before'. It denotes the act of homage before a monarch or a superior, or prostration before God in worship. For example, Jacob prostrates himself before his brother Esau (Gen. 33.3); Joseph's brothers do obeisance to Joseph, governor of Egypt (Gen. 42.6; 43.28); and various individuals make obeisance before King David.[1] In 1 Chronicles 29.20 the whole assembly (*ekklēsia*) 'worshipped (*prosekynēsan*) the Lord and the king'.[2] Obeisance is made before

---

[1] 2 Sam. 14.4, 22; 18.28; 1 Kings 1.23, 31.

[2] Could one speak properly of something equivalent to a '*ruler cult*' in Judaism? Cf. Horbury, *Jewish Messianism* 68–77, 114, 127–36. M. Barker, 'The High Priest and Worship of Jesus', in Newman, et al. (eds), *Jewish Roots* 93–111, presses the significance of 1 Chron. 29: 'the king was the visible presence of the Lord in the temple ritual and Solomon's enthronement was his apotheosis . . . this is what they meant by becoming divine' (94–5).

angelic beings;[3] and above all, obeisance is made before God.[4] Repeatedly, particularly in Deuteronomy and Isaiah, Israel is forbidden to make obeisance to any other gods or idols;[5] the Lord God alone was to be worshipped (Deut. 10.20).[6]

Similarly in the New Testament, Bauer-Danker defines *proskynein* as 'to express in attitude or gesture one's complete dependence on or submission to a high authority figure, so "(fall down and) worship, do obeisance to, prostrate oneself before, do reverence to, welcome respectfully"'.[7] The Greek term too is used in reference to human beings, the *proskynēsis* (the matching noun) signifying the acknowledgment of the person's sovereign power in relation to the one making the *proskynēsis*. So in Jesus' parable of the king settling his accounts with his slaves (Matt. 18.23–34) the slave falls down, prostrating himself before the king (18.26). Notably, two verses later, when the forgiven slave then threatens a fellow slave in his debt, the fellow slave 'falls down' but does not offer *proskynēsis* (18.29). In Mark's account of Jesus' humiliation by the Roman soldiers, 'they fell on their knees in homage (*prosekynoun*) to him', mocking the reverence that could have been his as 'king of the Jews' (Mark 15.18–20).[8] Strikingly, in his account of the conversion of the centurion Cornelius (Acts 10), Luke writes, 'falling at his [Peter's] feet, he [Cornelius] worshipped (*proskynēsen*) him'. Peter's response was to lift Cornelius to his feet and gently rebuke him: 'Stand up; I am only a human being' (10.25–26). In the letter to Philadelphia in Revelation 3, the promise is made that their opponents will

---

[3] Gen. 19.1; Num. 22.31; Josh. 5.14; *Joseph and Asenath* 15.11–12.

[4] Gen. 22.5; 24.26, 48, 52; Exod. 4.31; 12.27; 24.1; 33.10; 34.8; Deut. 10.20; 26.10; 32.43; etc.

[5] Exod. 20.5; 23.24; 34.14; Lev. 26.1; Deut. 4.19; 5.9; 8.19; 11.16; 17.3; 29.26; 30.17; Isa. 2.8, 20; 44.15, 17, 19; 46.6; Jer. 1.16; 8.2; 25.6; Mic. 5.13.

[6] Though Bauckham notes that the word 'is not employed in most Jewish worship' (*Jesus and the God of Israel* 204).

[7] BDAG 882.

[8] Hurtado regards it as 'mocking worship . . . probably to be taken ironically as unwittingly correct' (*How on Earth* 158 n. 21); though in reference to 'king of the Jews' NRSV is probably correct in regarding the *proskynēsis* in this case as 'homage'. It may also be relevant that 'king of the Jews' was not a title used for Jesus by the first Christians.

prostrate (*proskynēsousin*) themselves before the Philadelphians' feet (Rev. 3.9). The probability is that we should read the accounts of various individuals coming and prostrating themselves before Jesus during his mission in Galilee in the same light: the leper coming to Jesus for his help, prostrating himself (*proskynei*) before Jesus (Matt. 8.2); the ruler of the synagogue (Jairus) similarly bowing down before Jesus (*proskynei*) to ask for his help (Matt. 9.18); the Syrophoenician woman making similar appeal on behalf of her daughter (again *proskynei*) (Matt. 15.25); and the mother of the disciples James and John similarly falling before Jesus (*proskynousa*) to petition him on behalf of her sons (Matt. 20.20).[9]

In all these cases *proskynein* clearly implies the appropriate mode for making a petition to one of high authority who could exercise power to benefit the petitioner. That the power could be and probably was thought of as heavenly power in most of the cases cited did not carry with it the implication that the one who exercised the power was divine (note again Peter's gentle rebuke of Cornelius). But the authority and power was due the deepest respect, the petitioners evidently regarded themselves as wholly dependent on the favour of the one petitioned, and the obeisance expressed that depth of respect and sense of complete dependence.

More typically in the New Testament, *proskynein* is used of the worship (prostration) due to God, and to God alone. We should recall once again the rebuke of Jesus to the tempter: '(You shall) worship (*proskynēseis*) the Lord your God, and him only shall you serve' (Matt. 4.10/Luke 4.8).[10] In John's Gospel Jesus looks for a time when people will worship (*proskynēsousin*) God, the Father, in Spirit and in truth (John 4.21–24). In Acts we hear of the Ethiopian eunuch who had come to Jerusalem to worship (*proskynēsōn*) the God of Israel (Acts 8.27). Paul

---

[9] Other references in Matt. 14.33 and Mark 5.6 (demonically inspired words), and John 9.38 may have fuller significance for the Evangelists. See particularly Hurtado, *How on Earth* 158 n. 21, 159.

[10] MT/LXX say 'fear', not 'worship'; the scripture is modified or alternatively worded to match more closely to the words of the tempter.

looks for incomers to the assembly of believers to 'fall on their faces and worship God' (1 Cor. 14.25). And in the Revelation of John, God is regularly the focus of worship (*proskynein*).[11] Moreover, it is not only false worship of the beast that is rebuked,[12] but also any worship of other than God: the interpreting angel explicitly rebukes *proskynēsis* offered to him by the seer, and says emphatically, 'Worship (*proskynēson*) God' (Rev. 19.10; 22.8–9).

There are a few other occasions in the New Testament where *proskynein* is used with Jesus as the object. Curiously, though, these seem to move well beyond the sense of someone acknowledging the authority of someone of higher status. Very striking is the way Hebrews takes Moses' summons, 'Let all God's angels worship (*proskynēsatōsan*) him' (Deut. 32.43), and refers it to Christ (Heb. 1.6). Otherwise all the New Testament references to worshipping (*proskynein*) Jesus appear in the Gospels, principally Matthew, though only at Jesus' birth and after Jesus' resurrection. Matthew, we recall, was the writer who used the term *proskynein* most frequently in reference to several of Jesus' encounters. But he also uses the term to denote the worship or homage that the wise men brought to the recently born Jesus (Matt. 2.2, 8, 11). And he uses the same term in describing how the women who first encountered the risen Jesus took hold of his feet and worshipped (*proskynēsan*) him (Matt. 28.9). In the closing scene he similarly recounts that the remaining eleven disciples, when they saw Jesus in Galilee, 'worshipped (*prosekynēsan*) him, though some doubted' (28.17).[13] Luke had

---

[11] Rev. 4.10; 5.14; 7.11–12; 11.1, 16; 14.7; 15.3–4; 19.4, 10; 22.8–9.

[12] Rev. 13.4, 8, 12, 15; 16.2; 19.20; 20.4.

[13] Bauckham thinks that whereas in Mark and Luke the gesture of obeisance to Jesus was probably no more than a mark of respect for an honoured teacher, Matthew's consistent use of the word *proskynein* shows 'that he intends a kind of reverence which, paid to another human being, he would have regarded as idolatrous' – referring particularly to Matthew's unparalleled uses in epiphanic contexts (Matt. 2.2, 8, 11; 14.33; 28.9, 17), usage that 'must reflect the practice of the worship of Jesus in the church' (*Jesus and the God of Israel* 130–1). Similarly Hurtado, *How on Earth* 142–51, 158–9; his earlier *Origins* 66–8 does not press the case, bearing in mind the diversity of reverence that *proskynēsis* can express.

used the term only in his account of Jesus' temptations (Luke 4.7–8), and his use of it in the final sentence of his Gospel is slightly odd; there is some uncertainty as to what Luke actually wrote (NRSV margin),[14] and, as it stands, the text describes Jesus as carried up to heaven before 'they [the disciples] worshipped (*proskynēsantes*) him and returned to Jerusalem . . .' (Luke 24.52). Finally, even though the book of Revelation is consistent in talking of worship (*proskynein*) of God, we should add that in Revelation 5.14 the Lamb is surely included in the worship offered to 'the one seated on the throne and to the Lamb'.[15]

This is indeed intriguing. The number of references to Jesus being worshipped (*proskynein*) is surprisingly few. The clearest example is of worship offered to Jesus after his resurrection. And although the book of Revelation clearly envisions Jesus (the Lamb) being worshipped (Rev. 5), even the seer prefers to limit his use of *proskynein* to false worship of the beast and to the worship that should be given to God. Should we say to God alone? Presumably not, given the status of the Lamb. But this is an issue to which we will have to return. In any event, the use of *proskynein* in the sense of offering worship to Jesus seems to be rather limited. And there is a hint of uncertainty or hesitation as to whether this is the appropriate way to speak of the reverence due to Jesus.

However, this is only the beginning of our inquiry.

1.2 Other vocabulary

Other Greek words are sometimes translated as 'worship'.

(a) A close parallel to *proskynein* is the phrase 'to fall down', sometimes with the added phrases 'on one's face' or 'at the feet of'. The phrase sometimes accompanies *proskynein*, as in Matthew 2.11 (the wise men 'fell down and worshipped him [the infant Jesus]') and Revelation 5.8, 14 (in the seer's vision

---

[14] See e.g. the margins of NRSV, NJB and REB.
[15] In Rev. 15.3–4, however, the song of the Lamb, like the song of Moses, is sung to 'Lord God, the Almighty'; and in 19.10 the reference to Jesus is to 'the testimony of Jesus'.

'the elders fell down', or 'fell down and worshipped' the Lamb).[16] In Matthew 17.6 the disciples fall to the ground on the mount of transfiguration when the heavenly voice declares, 'This is my Son, the beloved.' Various individuals fall at Jesus' feet in appealing to him or thanking him (Mark 5.22/Luke 8.41; Luke 5.12; 17.16). In John 11.32 Mary (of Bethany) fell at Jesus' feet. In the Garden of Gethsemane Jesus throws himself to the ground in prayer (Mark 14.35/Matt. 26.39). In short, the action of 'falling at one's feet' denotes an appeal or submission to a higher power, as when the slave falls down before his king (Matt. 18.26), more than worship as such (which is why the word 'worship' is so often added). The phrase adds little or nothing to the use of *proskynein*.[17]

(b) The most common of the other near synonyms is *latreuein*, which basically means 'to serve'. In biblical literature, however, the reference is always to religious service, the carrying out of religious duties, 'to render cultic service'. So it is not surprising that it appears in conjunction with *proskynein* in (once again) Jesus' reply to the temptation to worship other than God: '(You shall) worship the Lord your God and (shall) serve (*latreuseis*) only him' (Matt. 4.10/Luke 4.8). And in several passages *latreuein* is translated 'worship' in English translations.[18] It is noticeable that in each case the object of the verb, the one who is (to be) served/worshipped, is God. Apart from one or two references to false worship,[19] the reference is always to the cultic service/worship of God.[20] In no case in the New Testament is there talk of offering cultic worship (*latreuein*) to Jesus. In this connection, the two references in the early Pauline

---

[16] Also Matt. 4.9; 18.26, 29; 1 Cor. 14.25; Rev. 4.10; 5.14; 7.11; 11.16; 19.4, 10; 22.8.

[17] See also Hurtado, *How on Earth* 139–41.

[18] Luke 2.37 (NRSV, NIV, REB); Acts 7.7, 42; 24.14 (NRSV, NIV, REB, NJB); 26.7 (NRSV, REB, NJB); 27.23 (NRSV, REB); Phil. 3.3 (NRSV, NIV, REB, NJB); 2 Tim. 1.3 (NRSV, REB); Heb. 8.5 (NRSV); 9.9 (NRSV, NIV, REB, NJB); 9.14 (NRSV, NJB); 10.2 and 12.28 (NRSV, NIV, REB, NJB); Rev. 7.15 (NRSV, REB); and 22.3 (NRSV, REB, NJB).

[19] Acts 7.42 (the host of heaven); Rom. 1.25 (the creature rather than the Creator).

[20] All the references in n. 18, above; and the remaining NT references – Luke 1.74; Rom. 1.9; Heb. 13.10.

letters are of some interest. In Romans 1.9 Paul calls on 'God as my witness whom I serve/worship (*latreuō*) with my spirit in the gospel of his Son'. And in Philippians 3.3 he speaks of Christians generally 'worshipping (*latreuontes*) by the Spirit of God and boasting in Christ Jesus'.

As with *latreuein*, so also with the matching noun, *latreia*, '(cultic) service, worship'. It refers always to the worship of God.[21] The most interesting example for us is again from Paul: 'I appeal to you, therefore, brothers, by the mercies of God, that you present your bodies as a living sacrifice, holy and acceptable to God, which is your spiritual worship (*latreian*).' The verse is of considerable interest and we will have to return to it. Here we need simply note that the number of *latreia* references is very limited, and here too the 'service/worship' is never thought of as offered to Jesus.

Here we should also mention the infrequent *leitourgein*, 'to render cultic worship' (as in Heb. 10.11, and in a variant reading of Titus 1.9),[22] but also 'to render material service', as in the giving to the collection that Paul was making for the poor in Jerusalem (Rom. 15.27).[23] But most interesting for us is Acts 13.2, where Luke describes the church in Antioch 'worshipping (*leitourgountōn*) the Lord'. Is 'the Lord' here Jesus (as frequently in Acts)?[24] Or does Luke speak of the worship of the Lord God?[25] It is difficult to decide, although, as in the other 'Lord' = God references in Acts, the influence of Old Testament usage suggests that Luke was thinking of worship of God.[26]

---

[21] John 16.2; Rom. 9.4; 12.1; Heb. 9.1, 6.

[22] As also the noun, *leitourgia*, in Luke 1.23; see also Phil. 2.17; Heb. 8.6; 9.21.

[23] As with the noun *leitourgia* in 2 Cor. 9.12; similarly Phil. 2.30.

[24] Note particularly Acts 1.21; 2.36; 9.1, 27, 28; 10.36; 11.24; 13.12; 14.23. Bauckham assumes 'the Lord' in Acts 13.2 is Jesus (*Jesus and the God of Israel* 129).

[25] As in Acts 1.24; 2.39; 3.20, 22; 4.26, 29; 12.23; 17.24.

[26] E. Haenchen, *The Acts of the Apostles* (ET Oxford: Blackwell, 1971) notes that 'Luke has borrowed an expression of special solemnity from LXX', citing 2 Chron. 5.14; 13.10; 35.3; Judith 4.14; Joel 1.13; 2.17; Ezek. 40.46; 44.16; 45.4; Dan. 7.10 (395 and n. 3). I discuss the whole issue at length in '*KYRIOS* in Acts', in C. Landmesser, et al. (eds), *Jesus Christus als die Mitte der Schrift*; Otfried Hofius FS (BZNW 86; Berlin: de Gruyter, 1997) 363–78, where I note that many references are ambiguous.

Thrēskeia, defined as the 'expression of devotion to transcendent beings, esp. as it expresses itself in cultic rites, [so] "worship"',[27] likewise denotes service offered to God – explicitly in James 1.26–27, by implication in Acts 26.5, and probably in Colossians 2.18.[28]

Bearing in mind that the *latreuein* word group is the nearest expression for the offering of 'cultic worship', the fact that it is never used for the 'cultic devotion' of Christ in the New Testament is somewhat surprising for Hurtado's main thesis and should be given some attention.[29]

(c) A significant term is *epikaleisthai*, 'to call upon'. It could be regarded as primarily a term for prayer (and so treated more appropriately in Chapter 2). But in its wide usage it signifies in effect worship as 'calling upon God'. In the Hebrew Bible (Old Testament) *qārā'* is regularly used 'to denote the establishment of a relation between a human individual and God . . . it is the verbal appeal for the deity's presence that is foundational to all acts of prayer and worship'.[30] In common Greek too *epikaleisthai* is regularly used of calling upon a deity.[31] So it is not surprising that the Septuagint uses the phrase frequently, *epikaleisthai to onoma kyriou* ('to call upon the name of the Lord'), that is in prayer.[32] The same usage naturally reappears

---

[27] BDAG 459.

[28] Col. 2.18 could refer to worship offered to angels, but more likely refers to angelic worship of God; see my *Colossians and Philemon* (NIGTC; Grand Rapids: Eerdmans, 1996) 179–82.

[29] Hurtado recognizes the exclusive God reference for *latreuein* and *latreia* but does not comment further (*Origins* 65). J. L. North, 'Jesus and Worship, God and Sacrifice', in Stuckenbruck and North (eds), *Early Jewish and Christian Monotheism* 186–202, notes that in distinguishing various kinds of worship (*proskynēsis*) John of Damascus reserved *latreia* as the special word to be used only for the unique worship of God (194–5).

[30] F. L. Hossfeld and E.-M. Kindl, '*qārā*', *TDOT* 13.113–15.

[31] BDAG 373. Alan Segal, 'Paul's "*SOMA PNEUMATIKON*" and the Worship of Jesus', in Newman, et al. (eds), *Jewish Roots* 258–76, notes that the terminology is characteristic both of pagan magic and of Jewish mystical texts: 'In the Hekhaloth texts, all kinds of angelic beings are invoked with the terminology' (274).

[32] See K. L. Schmidt, *TDNT* 3.499–500.

in the New Testament, where invocation of God is in view.[33] More striking, however, is the fact that it is the Lord Jesus who is 'called upon' on several occasions.[34] And even more striking is the fact that believers can be denoted simply as 'those who call upon the name of the Lord Jesus Christ' (1 Cor. 1.2).[35] The defining feature of these early Christians ('those who call upon the name of the Lord Jesus Christ' is almost a definition, equivalent to 'Christians') marked them out from others who 'called upon (the name of)' some other deity or heavenly being.[36] Moreover, in a still more striking passage, Paul refers Joel 3.5 (in the Septuagint) to Jesus: 'everyone who calls upon the name of the Lord will be saved' (Rom. 10.13), where it is clear from the context that 'the Lord' is the Lord Jesus (10.9).[37] We will have to return to this passage in Chapter 4. Here we need simply note that the same language, calling upon a deity, calling upon the Lord God, is used of Christ, and as a distinguishing characteristic of the earliest believers.

(d) Another term widely used in the ancient world with the meaning 'to worship' was *sebein*. So in Acts 19.27 it is used of

---

[33] Acts 2.21; 1 Pet. 1.17; cf. 2 Cor. 1.23.

[34] Acts 7.59 (Stephen); Rom. 10.12, 14; 2 Tim. 2.22.

[35] Also Acts 9.14, 21; 22.16; 2 Tim. 2.22.

[36] Both Hurtado (*Origins* 78–9; *Lord Jesus Christ* 198–9) and Bauckham (*Jesus and the God of Israel* 129–30) see these texts (1 Cor. 1.2; etc.) as evidence of 'cultic devotion' rendered to Jesus from 'very early moments of the Christian movement'. In contrast, P. M. Casey, 'Monotheism, Worship and Christological Development in the Pauline Churches', in Newman, et al. (eds), *Jewish Roots* 214–33, infers that what Paul had in mind was 'primarily the use of acclamations and confessions such as *maranatha* and *kyrios Iēsous*' (225). Hurtado adds the use of Jesus' name in baptism and healings/exorcisms as supporting evidence for his proposal 'that the early Christian use of Jesus' name represents a novel adaptation of [the] Jewish monotheistic concern [to maintain the uniqueness of the one God]' (200–6; here 204). He comments similarly on 1 Cor. 5.1–5, that the disciplinary action referred to there 'likely included a ritual invocation of Jesus' name and power to effect it. Jesus' cultic presence and power clearly operate here in the manner we otherwise associate with a god' (*Origins* 80).

[37] Similarly it can be argued that since in the Pentecost speech of Acts 2 Jesus has been made Lord (2.36), the calling on the name of the Lord in 2.17 refers also to cultic reverence/acclamation/invocation of the exalted Jesus (Hurtado, *Lord Jesus Christ* 179, 181).

the worship universally offered to 'the great goddess Artemis'. The word occurs once in the Gospels, when Jesus quotes God rebuking Israel through Isaiah the prophet (Isa. 29.13): 'In vain do they worship (*sebontai*) me, teaching human precepts as doctrines' (Matt. 15.9/Mark 7.7). In Acts it is mostly used of pious Gentiles who worshipped God, that is Gentiles who had been attracted by the religion of the Jews and who had attached themselves in some measure to the Jewish synagogue community. In current literature on the subject they are usually referred to as 'God-worshippers' or 'God-fearers'.[38] The most interesting reference for us, however, is Acts 18.13, where the Jews of Corinth bring a complaint against the proconsul: 'This man is persuading people to worship (*sebesthai*) God in ways that are contrary to the law'. Here again, apart from Acts 19.27, only worship of the God of Israel is in view.

(e) The correlative term *eusebein* means 'to show uncommon reverence or respect' for someone. In reference to God or gods it conveys the sense of 'worship'. So in Acts 17.23, Paul begins his speech to the Areopagus in Athens by referring to an altar 'to an unknown god', declaring, 'what therefore you worship (*eusebeite*) as unknown, this I proclaim to you'. In the only other New Testament reference, however, the verb is used of the respect that children owe to (other members of) their own family (1 Tim. 5.4). This term is of little help in our inquiry.[39]

From this brief survey of other terms for worship, including the term most appropriate for 'cultic worship', we have discovered that the writers of the New Testament have only worship of God in view as desirable and commendable. In this they are faithful to the teaching of their scriptures. The one real exception, and a significant exception, is their description of the

---

[38] Acts 13.43, 50; 16.14; 17.4, 17; 18.7; see also John 9.31 and 1 Tim. 2.10. On the subject of 'God-fearers' see my *Beginning from Jerusalem* (Grand Rapids: Eerdmans, 2009) 560–3.

[39] The same is true of the matching noun, *eusebeia*, which is used consistently in the sense of 'godliness, devoutness, piety', though never explicitly with the object of the devoutness indicated (Acts 3.12; 1 Tim. 2.2; 3.16; 4.7, 8; 6.3, 5, 6, 11; 2 Tim. 3.5; Titus 1.1; 2 Pet. 1.3, 6, 7; 3.11).

first Christians as 'those who call upon the name of the Lord Jesus Christ'.

1.3 Related terms

There are other terms that are regularly linked with the term 'worship' or carry the same implication. For example, in the *Gloria* of the traditional Christian liturgy, the worshippers say, 'we praise you, we bless you, we worship you, we glorify you; we give you thanks',[40] all, it should be noted, echoing the angels' worship of God in Luke 2.14, before (in the *Gloria*) attention is turned to Christ. So we should look also at whom the New Testament writers 'praised', whom they 'blessed', to whom they 'gave glory', or 'glorified', and to whom they 'gave thanks' in their worship.

We also need to bear in mind once again the long debate within early Catholic tradition as to the appropriate language to use in calling upon the saints. The logic was that since the saints are close to God (because they are 'saints', notably holy persons) their intercession on behalf of the Church on earth would be especially effective. The outcome was a distinction between language appropriate for approach to God, and language that could be used in appealing to the saints. 'Adoration' (Latin, *adoratio*; Greek, *latreia*) was due to God alone; but 'veneration' (Latin, *veneratio*; Greek, *douleia*) could be offered to the saints. In other words, Christian tradition envisaged different grades or degrees of worship, or reverence or devotion, and accepted that a form of worship might be offered to other than God alone.[41] I well recall one conversation that I had with a young Roman Catholic training for the priesthood, when my wife and I lived for some enjoyable weeks in the Venerable English College for trainee priests in Rome. I had attended an evening prayer in honour of the Virgin Mary, and as we exited I commented to the young man that I supposed the congregation

---

[40] Laudamus te, benedicimus te, adoramus te, glorificamus te; gratias agimus tibi.
[41] See e.g. the article on 'Saints, devotion to', in *ODCC* 1444–5.

had been venerating Mary, not worshipping her. 'No,' he replied; 'we worship her but do not adore her.'

So, what do the New Testament writers say about this further range of language relating to worship?

(a) We begin by noting that several of these further terms hardly feature in the New Testament at all. *Latreia* we have already looked at; 'adore'/'adoration' does not appear in English translations of the New Testament. Nor does the word 'venerate'. *Douleia* occurs only in the sense of 'slavery, servility', and always in a negative sense – the slavery to physical corruption (Rom. 8.21), slavery to the law (Gal. 5.1), slavery to the fear of death (Heb. 2.15).[42] The usage of the New Testament, of course, does not debar the later usage and distinctions. But in our attempt to ascertain the New Testament understanding of worship the later language of 'adoration' and 'veneration', and the distinction between them, are not helpful.

(b) The result is only slightly more positive with the terms 'revere' and 'reverence'. For they are appropriate translations in some cases for the Greek *phobein* ('to fear') and *phobos* ('fear'). The problem (if that is the right way to put it) is that both terms are used for quite a range of 'fear'. They can refer to fear of other people,[43] or of some eventuality such as death,[44] to a slave's respect for his master (Eph. 6.5; 1 Pet. 2.18), or to a wife's reverence for her husband (Eph. 5.33; 1 Pet. 3.2), as well as to fear of God.[45] For us the most interesting instance is Ephesians 5.21, 'Be subject to one another out of reverence (*phobō*) for Christ.' Although it is an isolated case, the sense is clearly that of a reverential fear of Christ, a usage entirely appropriate within a context of worship.

(c) We might have expected much more light from the language of 'praise', but it does not take us much further. The Greek terms, *ainein* and *epainein*, do not occur very frequently in the

---

[42] The only other NT references are Rom. 8.15 and Gal. 4.24.

[43] E.g. Matt. 14.5; Mark 6.20; John 9.22; Rom. 13.1; Gal. 2.12.

[44] Heb. 2.15. See further BDAG 1061–2.

[45] Luke 1.50; 18.2, 4; Acts 9.31; 10.35; 13.16, 26; Rom. 3.18; 2 Cor. 5.11; 7.1; Col. 3.22; 1 Pet. 2.17; Rev. 11.18; 14.7; 19.5.

New Testament. *Ainein* is used only of praise of God;[46] and *epainein* is usually used of praise of other individuals.[47] The noun *epainos* usually denotes approval or praise for individuals, including praise from God,[48] but it is certainly used for praise of God on a number of occasions (Eph. 1.6, 12, 14; Phil. 1.11). What is noteworthy about these latter instances is the way Christ features in them: the praise is for the grace bestowed on us in the Beloved (Eph. 1.6); God's purpose is that 'we should live for the praise of his glory, [we] who have already hoped in Christ' (Eph. 1.12);[49] the believers have 'produced the harvest of righteousness that comes through Jesus Christ for the glory and praise of God' (Phil. 1.11). Here again we notice that 'praise' is never offered to Jesus, though what he has done is certainly the cause of and occasion for praise of God.

(d) The regular term for 'give thanks to' is *eucharistein*, with the noun, *eucharistia,* often meaning 'the rendering of thanks, thanksgiving'. The verb is regularly used for giving thanks to God, as classically in the meals over which Jesus presided,[50] and other meals including the Lord's Supper.[51] That the thanks in prayers are directed to God is usually clear and mostly explicit.[52] The one exception is where the Samaritan leper healed by Jesus returns, falls on his face at Jesus' feet and thanks him (Luke 17.16), though this is probably more like the thanks to particular individuals for a service rendered (the leper's healing), as in Paul's thanksgiving to Prisca and Aquila in Romans 16.4. Noteworthy also are Colossians 3.17 and Ephesians 5.20, where thanks are

---

[46] Luke 2.13, 20; 18.43; 19.37; Acts 2.47; 3.8, 9; Rom. 15.11; Rev. 19.5. So too *ainesis* ('praise') – Heb. 13.15; and *hymnein* – Mark 14.26/Matt. 26.30; Acts 16.25; Col. 3.16; Heb. 2.12.

[47] Luke 16.8; 1 Cor. 11.2, 17, 22.

[48] Rom. 2.29; 13.3; 1 Cor. 4.5; 2 Cor. 8.18; 1 Pet. 1.7; 2.14.

[49] The order of the Greek indicates that the 'his glory' is the glory of God.

[50] Mark 8.6/Matt. 15.36; Mark 14.23 pars.; John 6.11, 23.

[51] Acts 27.35; Rom. 14.6; 1 Cor. 10.30; 11.24. Also *eucharistia* – 1 Tim. 4.3, 4.

[52] Luke 18.11; John 11.41; Acts 28.15; Rom. 1.8, 21; 1 Cor. 1.4, 14; 14.17, 18; Eph. 1.16; 5.20; Phil. 1.3; Col. 1.3, 12, 17; 1 Thess. 1.2; 2.13; 2 Thess. 1.3; 2.13; Philem. 4; Rev. 11.17. Less explicitly (but implicitly) with *eucharistia* – 1 Cor. 14.16; 2 Cor. 4.15; 9.11–12; Phil. 4.6; Col. 2.7; 4.2; 1 Thess. 3.9; 1 Tim. 2.1; Rev. 4.9; 7.12.

given to God the Father 'in the name of our Lord Jesus [Christ]'.
To give thanks in everything is 'the will of God in Christ Jesus
for us' (1 Thess. 5.18). Otherwise, when the language is used
so often by Paul in particular, it is again striking that he never
'gives thanks [in prayer]' to Jesus.

The noun *charis*, meaning 'grace', can also be used to express
'thanks', gratitude for a generous or beneficent act, for example
in reference to a slave for his service (Luke 17.9), but more
typically to God for his overwhelming grace.[53] The only time
when the thanks are directed to Christ is in 1 Timothy 1.12 –
'I am grateful (*charin*) to Christ Jesus our Lord'. The fact that
the more typical liturgical form is not used ('Thanks be to . . .')
need not be significant, since Hebrews 12.28 uses the same
form in urging, 'Let us give thanks, through which we offer
worship (*latreuōmen*) that is acceptable to God . . .' More typical,
however, is the fact that thanks are regularly given *through*
Christ to God:

> I give thanks (*eucharistō*) to my God through Jesus Christ.
> (Rom. 1.8)

> Thanks be to God (*charis tō theō*) through Jesus Christ our
> Lord! (Rom. 7.25, NRSV)

> It is through him that we say the 'Amen' to God to his glory.
> (2 Cor. 1.20)

> Do everything in the name of the Lord Jesus, giving thanks to
> God the Father through him. (Col. 3.17, NRSV)

> To the only wise God, through Jesus Christ, to whom be the
> glory for ever! (Rom. 16.27, NRSV)

> To the only God our Saviour, through Jesus Christ our Lord, be
> glory . . . (Jude 25, NRSV)

---

[53] Rom. 6.17; 7.25; 1 Cor. 15.57; 2 Cor. 2.14; 8.16; 9.15; Col. 3.16; 2 Tim. 1.3.

... so that God may be glorified in all things through Jesus Christ. (1 Pet. 4.11, NRSV)

Compare those examples with 2 Corinthians 2.14: 'Thanks be to God (*tō theō charis*), who in Christ Jesus always leads us in triumphal procession.'[54]

So, once again the language of worship is used almost exclusively for God, though occasionally for Jesus. But a more common usage is the giving of thanks to God *for* what Christ has done or *through* Christ or in the name of Christ.[55]

1.4 Doxologies

Characteristic worship language includes the terms *doxazein* 'to glorify', and to give glory (*doxa*) to. Once again the terms can be used in the sense of honouring someone else, as in Matthew 6.2, in reference to the 'hypocrites' who conduct themselves in the synagogues and streets 'in order that they might be praised (*doxasthōsin*) by others'. Similarly Jesus is 'praised (*doxazomenos*) by everyone' in his early Galilean mission (Luke 4.15). Paul can even glorify (*doxazō*) his own ministry as apostle to the Gentiles (Rom. 11.13), and can envisage members of the body (of Christ) being honoured (*doxazetai*) (1 Cor. 12.26). Nor should we forget that, for Paul in particular, the completion of the process of salvation is for those saved also to be glorified:[56] glory as the outcome of a life pleasing to God,[57]

---

[54] Hurtado notes that the two first-century writings among the Apostolic Fathers, *1 Clement* and *Didache*, both portray Jesus as the one through whom prayer is made to God, glory given to God, and God has made known the blessings of salvation (*Lord Jesus Christ* 615–17).

[55] Hurtado, *Origins* 95, quotes N. Richardson, *Paul's Language about God* (JSNTS 99; Sheffield Academic Press, 1993): 'God is always the object of Pauline thanksgivings, but the content is always explicitly or implicitly christological' – referring to 2 Cor. 8.16; Phil. 1.3; 1 Thess. 2.13; 3.9 (259).

[56] Rom. 8.18, 21, 30; 1 Cor. 2.7; 2 Cor. 3.18; 4.17; Gal. 1.5; Eph. 1.6, 18; 3.21; Phil. 3.21; Col. 1.27; 3.4; 2 Tim. 2.10; Heb. 2.10; 1 Pet. 1.7; 5.1, 4.

[57] Rom. 2.7, 10; 1 Pet. 5.4.

the restoration of what was lost in the fall of humanity (Rom. 3.23), the hope of sharing in God's own glory.[58] Much the most common usage of *doxa*, however, concerns glorifying or giving glory to God in worship and gratitude.[59] In two passages the word of the Lord is also glorified (Acts 13.48; 2 Thess. 3.1). And notably, again, 1 Peter speaks of God being glorified in all things through Jesus Christ (1 Pet. 4.11), and of individuals glorifying God by (bearing) the name 'Christian' (4.16).

'Glory' is regularly associated with Jesus' exaltation and coming (again).[60] John's Gospel makes great play with the theme of Jesus' glory as glory of the only Son from the Father, already visible in his ministry,[61] as glory that had been Jesus' glory before his entry into the world,[62] and of Jesus' glorification as already happening in his crucifixion as well as in its sequel.[63] Notable is the emphasis that God is glorified in the Son of Man (John 12.31–32; 14.13; 17.1, 4), but also that Jesus is glorified in his disciples (17.10, 22). In Acts 7.55 Stephen sees the glory of God and Jesus standing at the right hand of God. Paul speaks of the crucifixion of 'the Lord of glory' (1 Cor. 2.8) and similarly laments the blindness that prevents so many from seeing 'the glory of Christ, who is the image of God' and 'the glory of God in the face of Jesus Christ' (2 Cor. 4.4, 6). He looks for 'the glory of Christ' as well as 'the glory of God' (8.19, 23). In the great hymnic poem that opens Ephesians, praise is offered repeatedly, for the glory of God's grace 'freely bestowed

---

[58] Rom. 5.2; 1 Thess. 2.12; 1 Pet. 5.10.

[59] *Doxazein* – Matt. 5.16; 9.8; 15.31; Mark 2.12; Luke 2.20; 5.25, 26; 7.16; 13.13; 17.15; John 21.19; Acts 4.21; 11.18; 21.10; Rom. 1.21; 15.6, 9; 1 Cor. 6.20; 2 Cor. 9.13; Gal. 1.24; 1 Pet. 2.12; 4.11, 16; Rev. 15.4. *Doxa* – Luke 17.18; John 9.24; 11.4, 40; 12.43; Acts 12.23; Rom. 1.23; 3.7, 23; 4.20; 11.36; 15.7; 1 Cor. 10.31; 15.43; 2 Cor. 1.20; 4.15; Phil. 1.11; 2.11; 4.20; 1 Tim. 1.17; Rev. 1.6; 4.9, 11; 7.12; 11.13; 14.7; 16.9; 19.1, 7.

[60] Mark 8.38 pars.; 13.26 pars.; Matt. 19.28; 25.31; Luke 24.26; Acts 3.13; 1 Tim. 3.16; Titus 2.13; Heb. 2.9; Jas. 2.1; 1 Pet. 1.11, 21.

[61] John 1.14; 2.11; 17.22, 24. Similar is Heb. 1.3 – God's Son as 'the reflection of God's glory'.

[62] John 12.41; 17.5; see further in Ch. 4, below.

[63] John 7.39; 8.54; 12.16, 23, 28; 16.14; 17.1, 5.

on us in the Beloved', for 'his [Christ's] glory', and for 'his [God's] glory' (Eph. 1.6, 12, 14), as all of a piece. And the first half of the letter ends with the ascription 'to him [God] be glory in the church and in Christ Jesus to all generations for ever and ever' (3.21). The more famous hymn of Philippians 2.6–11 climaxes with the hope of every tongue confessing 'Jesus Christ is Lord, to the glory of God the Father' (2.11). And the letter ends with the reassurance that 'God will satisfy your every need according to his riches in glory in Christ Jesus' (4.19). In 2 Thessalonians 2.14 the hope is to 'obtain the glory of our Lord Jesus Christ'. Titus 2.13 speaks of 'the appearing of the glory of our great God and Saviour Jesus Christ'. Doxologies addressed to Christ alone ('To him be glory for ever and ever') are rare, but do appear within the New Testament,[64] while in Jude 25 glory is given 'to the only God our Saviour, through Jesus Christ our Lord'.

What is striking in all this is the consistent thought of Jesus sharing in God's glory, manifesting that glory in his mission on earth, as embodying God's glory, and as the chief means and agent of God's purpose to restore his creation to glory, the glory of Christ's own resurrection and exaltation. The liturgical ascription ('Glory to Christ') as such may appear only in writings usually dated among the later documents of the New Testament, but the association of Christ with God's glory seems to be consistent across the New Testament, and the conviction that the exalted Christ shares in God's glory, and should be glorified with God or to the glory of God, is part of Christianity's distinctive foundation. Understandably Bauckham affirms that 'the attribution of doxologies to Christ is particularly clear evidence of unambiguously divine worship, i.e. worship that is appropriately offered only to the one God'; and he concludes that 'there could be no more explicit way of expressing

---

[64] 2 Tim. 4.18; 2 Pet. 3.18; also Rev. 5.12. In Rev. 5.13 the doxology is addressed both to 'the one who is seated on the throne' and to 'the Lamb'. Bauckham thinks it not very likely that Heb. 13.21 and 1 Pet. 4.11 are addressed to Christ (*Jesus and the God of Israel* 133).

divine worship of Jesus than in the form of a doxology addressed to him'.[65]

1.5 The language of benediction

A characteristic feature of Jewish prayer is to bless the Lord God for his goodness and as the God of Israel. We find this regularly in the Psalms: 'Blessed be the Lord, for he has heard the sound of my pleadings' (Ps. 28.6); 'Blessed be the Lord, for he has wondrously shown his steadfast love to me' (31.21); 'Blessed be the Lord, the God of Israel, from everlasting to everlasting' (41.13); and so on.[66] The usage is deeply rooted in Scripture.[67] And the famous Jewish prayer, the Eighteen Benedictions (*Shemoneh 'Esreh*), concludes each prayer with a benediction, 'Blessed art thou, Lord . . .': 'Blessed art thou, Lord, shield of Abraham'; 'Blessed art thou, Lord, who makest the dead alive'; and so on. The form and character of the prayer were probably already familiar at the time of Jesus.[68] So the language of benediction was very familiar to the first Christians.[69]

In Greek the blessing could be pronounced using *makarios, eulogia* or *eulogētos*. The first Christians made little use of the first in speaking of God as 'blessed' (1 Tim. 1.11; 6.15), and most Christians will be more familiar with the word used of the privileged or happy state of beneficiaries of divine blessing, as expressed most famously in the Beatitudes of Jesus (Matt. 5.3–12). *Eulogia* likewise is mostly used of a blessing received,

---

[65] Bauckham, *Jesus and the God of Israel* 132–3.

[66] See also Pss. 66.20; 68.19, 35; 72.18, 19; 89.52; 106.48; 118.26; 119.12; 124.6; 133.21; 144.1.

[67] Gen. 9.26; 14.20, 27; Exod. 19.10; Ruth 4.14; 1 Sam. 25.32, 39; etc.

[68] See further E. Schürer, *The History of the Jewish People in the Age of Jesus Christ* (ed. G. Vermes, et al., 4 vols; Edinburgh: T&T Clark, 1973–87) 2.455–9.

[69] In Tobit 11.14, Tobit expresses his praise thus: 'Blessed be God, and blessed be his great name, and blessed be all his holy angels.' See further L. T. Stuckenbruck, '"Angels" and "God": Exploring the Limits of Early Jewish Monotheism', in Stuckenbruck and North (eds), *Early Jewish and Christian Monotheism* 45–70 (here 56–60).

offered to, or bestowed upon individuals, though in Revelation it is used in the acclamations of both the Lamb and God (Rev. 5.12–13; 7.12).

Eulogētos, however, is used only to refer to 'the blessed one [God]' (Mark 14.61), or to ascribe blessedness to God: 'Blessed be the Lord God of Israel' (Luke 1.68); 'the Creator, who is blessed for ever' (Rom. 1.25); 'Blessed be the God and Father of our Lord Jesus Christ' (2 Cor. 1.3; 11.31; Eph. 1.3; 1 Pet. 1.3). Most intriguing of all is the benediction of Romans 9.5, which can be read either as '. . . the Christ according to the flesh, who is over all, God blessed for ever' or as '. . . the Christ according to the flesh. He who is God over all be blessed for ever.' This is a passage to which we shall have to return. Here we should just note that however Romans 9.5 is read, the more common and typical usage was to acclaim the blessedness of 'the God and Father of our Lord Jesus Christ'.

Also highly significant for us is the early Christian practice of beginning and ending letters to fellow Christians with a benediction or blessing. We know from the many papyrus letters (discovered from early in the twentieth century) how popular letters were written, and particularly how they followed the conventions of the initial greeting and the final farewell. These letters also make it possible for us to recognize both that Paul was aware of these conventions, and how he adapted them and forged his own conventions. Where, for example, the ordinary Greek letter would begin with a greeting, A to B *chairein* ('greeting'), Paul typically transformed the *chairein* into his favourite *charis* ('grace') and supplemented it with the characteristic Jewish greeting, *shalom = eirēnē* ('peace') – 'Grace and peace from God our Father and the Lord Jesus Christ'.[70] Likewise, whereas the typical letter of the time ended with a wish for the recipient's good health (*errōso, errōsthe*, 'be in good health, farewell'), Paul again typically ended with a formula

---

[70] Rom. 1.7; 1 Cor. 1.3; 2 Cor. 1.2; Gal. 1.3; Eph. 1.2; Phil. 1.2; Col. 1.2; 1 Thess. 1.1; 2 Thess. 1.2; 1 Tim. 1.2; 2 Tim. 1.2; Titus 1.4; Philem. 3; also 2 John 3; Rev. 1.4.

that recalled his greeting – 'The grace of our Lord Jesus Christ be with you'.[71]

There are two very striking features of this practice, apparently begun by Paul. One is that Paul had no hesitation in linking 'the Lord Jesus Christ' with 'God our Father' in formally praying for blessing on the recipients of his letters. The 'grace and peace' were conceived of as having a conjoint source: 'God our Father and the Lord Jesus Christ'.[72] Jesus as Lord was one with God in overseeing the spiritual wellbeing of the young Christians. The other remarkable feature is that the closing benediction takes it as given that grace, that is, of course, the grace of God, was also 'the grace of the Lord Jesus Christ'. The grace of God, already so fully expressed in creation and in the history of Israel, had now been summed up, most fully expressed and embodied in Jesus Christ. Christ could be called on as the fullest or most effective purveyor of God's grace.

1.6 Conclusion

In pursuing our question, 'Did the first Christians worship Jesus?', our inquiry into the language of worship initially turned up rather limited findings, at least so far as word statistics are concerned. 'Worship' as such is a term rarely used in reference to Christ. It appears most clearly in the wonder of the realization that God had raised Jesus from the dead, and in some of the worship offered to the Lamb in the visions of the seer of Revelation. Cultic worship or service (*latreuein, latreia*) as such is never offered to Christ, and other worship terms are used only in relation to God (including Acts 13.2?). In the case of the most common words for praise and thanksgiving (*eucharistein*), they too are never offered to Christ. More common is the

---

[71] Rom. 16.20; 1 Cor. 16.23; 2 Cor. 13.13; Gal. 6.18; Phil. 4.23; 1 Thess. 5.28; 2 Thess. 3.18; Philem. 25; also Rev. 22.21.

[72] 'Already well within the first two decades of the Christian movement it was common (and uncontroversial among believers) to include Jesus with God as source of the blessings invoked and appealed for in their devotional life' (Hurtado, *Origins* 75).

giving of thanks to God for what Jesus has done. In all this we would have to speak of something like a reserve or caution in the language of worship insofar as it was used in reference to Jesus. The first answer to our question, 'Did the first Christians worship Jesus?', would therefore seem to be, 'Generally no', or 'Only occasionally', or 'Only with some reserve.'

All the same, the fact that such worship language is used in reference to Jesus, even if only occasionally, is very striking. This would have been entirely unusual and without precedent in the Judaism of the time. For Christians to understand themselves and define themselves as 'those who invoke the name of the Lord Jesus Christ' in prayer must have marked them and their religious devotion as distinctive both within Palestine and in the wider Mediterranean world. The fact that this definition could be used as casually and as taken for granted, as it is in 1 Corinthians 1.2, assuredly indicates that invocation of the Lord Jesus in prayer was a regular feature of early Christian worship.

Moreover, as the inquiry proceeded, the initial picture became more complicated. For though the worship language, 'to glorify', is also used only of God, there is a consistent thought through the New Testament of Jesus sharing in the glory of God. The thought is not only of Jesus as the agent or embodiment of God's glory, but of glory as also being given to Jesus, as glory is given to God. And in the benedictions that begin and conclude Paul's letters, 'the Lord Jesus Christ' is presented equally with 'God our Father' as the source of grace and peace, and as the one through whom pre-eminently the grace of God has come and still comes to expression.

In reflecting further on how this relationship of the Lord Jesus Christ with God is conceived, we should recall also the repeated conviction that thanks to God are given 'through Jesus Christ' or 'in the name of our Lord Jesus', or that God is glorified or to be given glory 'through Jesus Christ'. Christ, in other words, seems to have been thought of as on both sides of the worship relationship – as in at least some degree the object of worship, but also as the enabler or medium of effective worship.

2

The practice of worship

The language of worship is only one of the areas to be examined if we are to find an answer to our question ('Did the first Christians worship Jesus?') that is both true to the worship of the first Christians and genuinely reflects the emphases and concerns of the New Testament writers. Equally important, perhaps more important, is the subject of how the first Christians *practised* worship. However they used the language of worship, did they *actually* worship Jesus? Did they express what Larry Hurtado has described as '*cultic devotion*' to Jesus? Indeed, it is Larry Hurtado's thorough discussion of the beginnings of christology and the origins of Christian worship that poses our question most clearly. For his finding is that 'Christ-devotion' or 'devotion to Jesus' was expressed from the very earliest days of Christianity.[1]

What devotional or cultic practice is in view? If we take one step back, what constituted the practice of worship at the time of Jesus? What did worshippers do? Turning once again to Jesus'

---

[1] See Introduction n. 3, above. Hurtado also emphasizes the importance of the pattern of early Christian devotional *practice* in his discussion (*How on Earth* 27). The main debate as to whether and when we can speak of 'a cult of Christ' began with W. Bousset, *Kyrios Christos* (1913, 1921; ET; Nashville: Abingdon, 1970), who maintained that cultic devotion to Jesus emerged as a consequence of his being designated *kyrios* ('Lord') in the Hellenistic Christian communities. Hurtado's aim was to revise Bousset by arguing that cultic devotion was already being expressed in the earlier/earliest Christian (Palestinian) communities. Horbury also denies that the cult of Christ had Gentile origins, but argues that the principal influence was Jewish messianism, including cultic honour paid to the king and to angels (*Jewish Messianism* Ch. 4). He also argues that the development of the Christ cult was influenced by the reverence paid to Israel's saints; 'The Cult of Christ and the Cult of the Saints', *NTS* 44 (1998) 444–69. His thesis is disputed with some effect by Hurtado, *Origins* 72–3 n. 23, and Bauckham, *Jesus and the God of Israel* 228–32.

reply to his tempter, '(You shall) worship the Lord your God, and him only shall you serve' (Matt. 4.10/Luke 4.8), to what practices was Jesus referring? The answer is that at the time of Jesus the practice of worship would have included at least four elements:

1 Prayer was obviously at the heart of worship[2] – as it is today, with the prayers of adoration, of penitence and confession, of petition and intercession, all indicating the dependence of the inferior (creature) upon the all-powerful Creator, Saviour and Lord.
2 Hymns sung to and in praise of God have equally been an expression of worship from time immemorial.
3 The setting aside of sacred space dedicated to the deity where the worship should be offered, the appointment of sacred individuals to transact the worship, and of sacred times for the cultic worship in the sanctuary have always been seen as integral to effective worship.
4 The surrender of material goods, dedicated to God, has also been fundamental. At the time of Jesus, the whole cult of sacrifice, including bloody sacrifice of animals, constituted the central act of cultic worship.

Our question can then be more precisely answered by asking whether cultic devotion in these terms was expressed or offered to Jesus by the first Christians. We will proceed by examining what the New Testament attests in relation to each of the four elements of worship outlined above.

2.1 Prayer

In the scriptures of Israel, we find regular references to prayer being offered to God. The phrase 'X prayed to the Lord',[3] or to

---

[2] It occasions no surprise that the term *proseuchē* ('prayer') was regularly used in the extended sense of 'prayer house' for synagogues or 'place of prayer'; see further BDAG 878–9; and my *Jesus Remembered* (Grand Rapids: Eerdmans, 2003) 304 n. 226.
[3] E.g. Num. 11.2; Deut. 9.26; 1 Sam. 1.10; 2 Kings 4.33; 2 Chron. 32.24; Isa. 37.15; Jer. 37.3; Dan. 9.4; Jonah 2.1.

God,[4] occurs frequently. It is assumed that only God is to be thus
'prayed' to.[5] And the importance of prayer to the Lord God is
indicated by the religious rules that developed to ensure that
the ritual prayer of worship was offered with due solemnity
and formality.[6]

In the New Testament the offering of prayer is described
in various ways. Let us now examine in sequence the terms
used and the praying they refer to, beginning with the
Gospels.

(a) The Gospels

The most common references to prayer involve the verb
proseuchesthai and the matching noun *proseuchē*. In the Synoptic
Gospels Jesus speaks on several occasions about praying
(*proseuchesthai*), with the assumption that prayer is made to
God. Among his best-known instructions on prayer are those
to pray privately and without heaping up empty phrases,
and the Lord's Prayer (Matt. 6.5–13/Luke 11.1–4). The Gospel
writers, particularly Luke, note that Jesus himself prayed
regularly, often going to a mountain or desert place to pray by
himself.[7] Matthew, Mark and Luke all make much of Jesus
praying in the Garden of Gethsemane, prior to his betrayal
(Mark 14.32–39 pars.).

The less prominent term *deesthai*, 'ask, request' can be used
both of requests to other individuals and of requests to God.
In the narratives of Matthew, Mark and Luke we find both

---

[4] Gen. 20.17; Job 33.26; Neh. 2.4; Pss. 5.2; 64.1.

[5] Though, curiously, Josephus reports that 'before the sun is up (the Essenes)
offer to him certain prayers (*euchas*), which have been handed down from
their forefathers, as though entreating him to rise' (*Jewish War* 2.133). This
tradition goes back at least to Ezek. 8.16, where Ezekiel reports seeing about
25 men, 'with their backs to the Temple, turned toward the east, prostrating
themselves to the sun toward the east'. Mishnah *Sukkah* 5.5 cites the same passage
disapprovingly.

[6] See e.g. E. Gerstenberger, *pll*, *TDOT* 11 (2001) 574–5.

[7] Matt. 14.23; Mark 1.35; 6.46; Luke 3.21; 5.16; 6.12; 9.18, 28–29; 11.1.

usages, with requests made to Jesus[8] and Jesus talking of making requests to God.[9]

Another word with a similar range of usage is *aitein*, 'to ask for'. In the same Gospels it is used, for example, of requests for the head of John the Baptist (Mark 6.22–25), of the crowd's asking for Barabbas (Matt. 27.20), and for Joseph's request for the body of Jesus (Mark 15.43 pars.). Presumably the request of James and John to Jesus for the top seats in his glory falls into the same category (Mark 10.35, 38). But Jesus also uses it of requests in prayer to God.[10]

A near synonym is *erōtan*, which also covers a range of requests – in the Gospels, asking someone a question,[11] or asking in the sense of requesting/inviting.[12]

Finally it should be noted that *parakalein* can be used in a range of senses – 'appeal to', 'urge, exhort, encourage', 'request, implore, entreat', or 'comfort, encourage, cheer up'. In the Gospels it appears usually in the sense of 'appeal, entreat' – various individuals entreating Jesus for help, or the Gerasenes entreating him to depart.[13] In one Synoptic passage Jesus uses the same word for an appeal to the Father, when he says that he could appeal to his Father and he would send more than twelve legions of angels to his assistance (Matt. 26.53).

John's Gospel uses none of the common words for prayer (*proseuchesthai, proseuchē, deesthai, deēsis*), but his use of *aitein* and *erōtan* is more adventurous. The Samaritan woman could have asked Jesus (*aitein*) for living water (John 4.10). Jesus promises to ask (*erōtan*) the Father to give his disciples another Advocate (14.16), and in his great prayer to the Father he asks

---

[8] Luke 5.12; 8.28, 38; 9.38 (the same request made to the disciples – 9.40).

[9] Matt. 9.38/Luke 10.2; Luke 21.36; 22.32 (Jesus makes a request on behalf of Simon Peter). The noun *deēsis* is used exclusively of requests made to God (Luke 1.13; 2.37; 5.33).

[10] Mark 11.24; Matt. 7.7–11/Luke 11.9–13; Matt. 6.8; 18.19.

[11] As in Matt. 16.13; 19.17; Matt. 21.24/Luke 20.3; Mark 4.10; 8.5; Luke 9.45; 19.31; 22.68; 23.3; John 1.19, 21, 25; 5.12; 8.7; 9.2, 15, 19, 21; 16.5; 18.19, 21.

[12] Luke 5.3; 7.36; 8.37; 11.37; John 4.40; 12.21; 19.31, 38.

[13] E.g. Mark 1.40; 5.17, 23; 7.32; 8.22.

(*erōtan*) on their behalf (17.9, 15, 20). He repeatedly promises that whatever his disciples ask (*aitein*) in his name the Father will give them (15.16; 16.23–24), even promising that he (himself) will do whatever his disciples ask (*aitein*) in his name, 'so that the Father may be glorified' (14.13). And he adds, 'If you ask me for anything in my name, I will do it' (14.14). Requests to the Father in Jesus' name are of a piece with requests to Jesus himself; the common factor is 'in his name'. 'In that day you will ask (*aitein*) in my name. I do not say to you that I will ask (*erōtan*) the Father on your behalf; for the Father himself loves you' (16.26–27). If the disciples abide in him and his words abide in them they may ask (*aitein*) whatever they want and it will be done for them (15.7).

(b) The rest of the New Testament

Elsewhere in the New Testament writings, 'prayer' as such (*proseuchesthai, proseuchē*), explicitly or implicitly, is always made to God.

Deesthai is used in the sense 'beg a favour' from someone else,[14] but also for a prayer request.[15] Interestingly in Acts 8.22, 24, where Simon is urged to 'pray (*deesthai*) to the Lord' that he might be forgiven, the reference to 'the Lord' is ambiguous.[16] But *deēsis* is used in the Epistles always for prayer; that is, prayer to God.

In Acts *aitein*, 'ask for', and *erōtan*, 'ask, request', appear mostly in everyday usage, though the request (*aitein*) is to God in Acts 7.46. But in the Epistles *aitein* is used almost exclusively in prayer contexts. For example, 'I pray (*aitoumai*) that you may not lose heart over my sufferings' (Eph. 3.13); God 'is able to accomplish abundantly far more than all we can ask (*aitoumetha*) or imagine' (3.20); 'we have not ceased praying (*proseuchomenoi*) for you and asking (*aitoumenoi*) that you may be filled with the knowledge of God's will' (Col. 1.9); those who lack faith should

---

14 Acts 8.34; 21.39; 26.3; 2 Cor. 5.20; 8.4; 10.2; Gal. 4.12.
15 Acts 4.31; 10.2; Rom. 1.10; 1 Thess. 3.10.
16 See Ch. 1 n. 26, above.

ask (*aitein*) God for it, but in faith (Jas. 1.5–6; similarly 4.2–3); 1 John similarly encourages its readers/audiences to ask (*aitein*) God boldly in prayer (1 John 5.14–16). And although *erōtan* appears in the Epistles usually in the everyday sense of 'ask, request', again in 1 John 5.16 the request is to God (on behalf of an erring brother). Yet, notably, when used in prayer, *aitein* and *erōtan* always refer to asking (for) or requesting addressed to God, and never to Jesus.

Parakalein throws up the most interesting example. In Acts and the Epistles it regularly appears in the everyday sense of 'urge, exhort'. For example, Paul exhorts the recipients of his letters, 'I urge/appeal to (*parakalō*) you',[17] and in 2 Corinthians he reflects twice and at some length on the thought of being 'comforted' (2 Cor. 1.3–7; 7.4–7, 13). The only obvious case of *parakalein* being used in a prayer context is 2 Corinthians 12. Paul speaks of the painful 'thorn in the flesh', which he calls 'a messenger of Satan to torment me'.

> Three times I appealed (*parekalesa*) to the Lord about this, that it would leave me, but he said to me, 'My grace is sufficient for you, for power is made perfect in weakness.' So, I will boast all the more gladly of my weaknesses, so that the power of Christ may dwell in me. (2 Cor. 12.8–9, NRSV)

What is so interesting here is not only the fact that *parakalein* is used in the sense of an 'appeal' made in prayer, but that it is evidently made to the Lord Jesus Christ. This can safely be concluded not simply because 'the Lord' in Paul is almost always the Lord Jesus (apart from its occurrence in scriptural quotations)[18] but also because the grace and power that the one appealed to promises Paul in answer to his appeal is specifically identified as 'the power of Christ'. Whatever else we

---

[17] Rom. 12.1; 15.30; 16.17; 1 Cor. 1.10; 4.16; 16.12, 15; 2 Cor. 2.8; 6.1; 9.5; 10.1; 12.18; Eph. 4.1; Phil. 4.2; 1 Thess. 4.1, 10; 5.14; 2 Thess. 3.12; 1 Tim. 1.3; 2.1; Titus 2.6; Philem. 9, 10; similarly Heb. 13.19, 22; 1 Pet. 2.11; 5.1; Jude 3.

[18] Though see further Ch. 4.2, below.

may conclude from the restricted language of prayer and request, then, it is clear enough that Paul understood the exalted Christ as one who could be appealed to for help, a request or petition that can readily be understood as prayer.[19]

Another passage that calls for attention is the closing paragraph of 1 Corinthians. There, in the midst of his final exhortations and benediction Paul inserts the Aramaic phrase '*Marana tha*' (1 Cor. 16.22; cf. Rev. 22.20). The fact that it appears in Aramaic strongly suggests that it had become a regular feature in early liturgies – rather like the continued use of the Aramaic '*Abba*, Father' in the prayers of the Greek-speaking churches (Rom. 8.15; Gal. 4.6). The Aramaic phrase in 1 Corinthians 16.22 should probably be translated, 'Our Lord, come'. Is this a prayer to Jesus? It certainly counts as an appeal made to the Jesus exalted to heaven that he should now come (again) from heaven – part of the intensive belief within earliest Christianity that Jesus would indeed (soon) return to earth.[20] Yet perhaps we should recall that according to the Gospels, when Jesus cried out on the cross, some of the bystanders thought he was calling on (*phōnei*) Elijah; that is calling for him to come and help him (Mark 15.35–36). Elijah, it should be remembered, had been taken to heaven without dying (2 Kings 2.11–12), and there was a widespread expectation that he would return from heaven before the day of the Lord.[21] However, we have no examples of appeals to Elijah being made in Second Temple Judaism for him to return or to help someone,[22] though we should also recall Alan Segal's observation that in Jewish mystical texts all kinds of angelic beings are invoked.[23] Nevertheless, if we take the account of Jesus' crucifixion seriously, it may provide evidence that the contemporaries of Jesus could well

---

[19] 'Paul's easy recounting of his actions suggests that he expects his readers to be familiar with prayer-appeals to Jesus as a communally accepted feature of Christian devotional practice' (Hurtado, *Origins* 75).

[20] See e.g. Acts 1.11; 3.19–21; 1 Cor. 15.51; 1 Thess. 4.15–17; Rev. 22.20.

[21] Mal. 4.5; cf. Mark 6.15; 8.28; John 1.21. See further Ch. 3.4(b).

[22] Hurtado, *Origins* 77.

[23] See Ch. 1 n. 31, above.

conceive of an appeal being made to one who had been translated to heaven that he come (again) to earth. Would that count
as a prayer, or as an appeal to one who had been exalted to
fulfil the hopes laid on him? Should we make such a distinction in any case?[24] It is not easy to reach a clear answer on such
questions.

Above all, however, we should recall what we noted in
Chapter 1 regarding the use of *epikaleisthai* ('to call upon') in
relation to Jesus. Here we may note the case of Stephen in his
dying moments: 'And they stoned Stephen, calling upon (*epika-
loumenon*) and saying, "Lord Jesus, receive my spirit"' (Acts
7.59). Nor should we forget the characterization of Christians
as 'those who call upon the name of the Lord Jesus Christ'
(1 Cor. 1.2). To call upon Jesus (in prayer) was evidently a
defining and distinguishing feature of earliest Christian
worship.[25] 1 Thessalonians, probably the earliest writing in the
New Testament, provides a good example of invocation of the
Lord Jesus (in the spirit of 1 Corinthians 16.22):

> Now may our God and Father himself and our Lord Jesus direct
> our way to you. And may the Lord make you increase and
> abound in love for one another and for all, just as we abound
> in love for you. And may he so strengthen your hearts in holi-
> ness that you may be blameless before our God and Father at
> the coming of our Lord Jesus with all his saints.
>
> (1 Thess. 3.11–13, NRSV)

And 2 Thessalonians has several examples of invocations to
the Lord: 'may the Lord comfort/direct/give you . . .' (2 Thess.
2.16–17; 3.5, 16).[26]

The conclusion to be drawn from this array of evidence, then,
is rather similar to the conclusion drawn from the first chapter.

---

[24] Casey questions how much can be drawn from 1 Cor. 16.22 ('Monotheism, Worship
and Christological Development in the Pauline Churches', in Newman, et al. (eds),
Jewish Roots 223–5).

[25] See also Ch. 1 n. 35, above.

[26] See also Hurtado, *Origins* 74–5. Fee deduces that Paul addressed prayer to Christ
as often as he did to God the Father (*Pauline Christology* 493–4).

The most explicit prayer language is used exclusively of prayer to God. Jesus himself is remembered as regularly praying to God and giving instruction on prayer to God. With the less explicitly prayer language of 'asking, requesting and appealing to' the picture is somewhat different. Again, where it appears in prayer, the request is normally addressed to God. But in John's Gospel repeated emphasis is placed by Jesus on his disciples' future praying to God 'in his [Jesus'] name'. Paul both appeals directly to Jesus for help from heaven and reflects a commonly used appeal for the Lord Christ to come (again) from heaven. And the earliest Christians are known as 'those who call upon or invoke the name of Jesus'.[27] If, speaking with tightly focused precision, 'prayer' as such was not usually made to Jesus in the worship of the first Christian congregations, at least he was regarded as one, sitting at God's right hand, who could be and was called upon, and to whom appeal could be made.[28] Was this more like an appeal to Elijah or like appeals that were later made to saints? Or should it be seen as a typical expression of earliest Christian worship? The answer is not quite so obvious or clear cut as we would like.[29]

---

[27] How different is 'invoking the name of Jesus' and praying 'in the name of Jesus'? Do both envisage prayer to God that names Jesus' name as giving the authorization necessary so to pray?

[28] Worth noting is the observation of J. A. Jungmann, *The Place of Christ in Liturgical Prayer* (London: Chapman, 1965): 'Looking back over the first centuries of the Christian era, we may come to this conclusion: to judge from all that survives in documents and accounts of the Church's life in this period, liturgical prayer, in regard to its form of address, keeps with considerable unanimity to the rule of turning to God (repeatedly described as the Father of Jesus Christ) through Christ the High Priest . . . It was not until the end of the fourth century that we meet by way of exception prayers to Christ the Lord, and these are not within the eucharistic celebration proper, but in the pre-Mass and in Baptism. On the other hand we know that in private prayers, both in apostolic times and later, the prayer to Christ was well known and customary' (164–6). This also reminds us that a more prominent theme in the NT is Jesus as the one who prays for his followers rather than the one prayed to (see further Ch. 4.6).

[29] Hurtado notes that in the NT 'any direct prayer or appeal to Christ is always to be framed by the sovereignty of the one God, and is in fact very limited in scope and frequency' (*Origins* 104); he is less inhibited in *Lord Jesus Christ* 138–40.

2.2 Hymns

The Psalms of the Old Testament can be regarded as typical of the hymns or songs sung by Israel in praise to God. From the Dead Sea Scrolls we also know that hymns and psalms continued to be written and sung as an integral part of the worship of God at Qumran in the period prior to Jesus.[30] The first Christians evidently followed the same practice. For example, before leaving the upper room to go to the Mount of Olives Jesus and the disciples 'sang a hymn' (Mark 14.26 par.); when jailed in Philippi Paul and Silas 'prayed and sang hymns to God' (Acts 16.25); and 'psalms, hymns and spiritual songs to God' were a regular part of Christian worship (Col. 3.16).[31] The parallel passage to Colossians 3.16 in Ephesians elaborates on Colossians by adding 'singing (*adontes*) and making melody (*psallontes*) to the Lord in your hearts, giving thanks (*eucharistountes*) to God the Father . . . in the name of our Lord Jesus Christ' (Eph. 5.19–20). Here 'the Lord' is presumably Christ; the thought of singing praise to Christ was obviously seen as of a piece with giving thanks to God in the name of Christ. And although it stretches the survey beyond the New Testament, we should also note the description that Pliny, the governor of Bithynia, gave to Emperor Trajan in about 112 CE, regarding the Christians he interrogated: 'it was their habit on a fixed day to assemble before the daylight and sing antiphonally a hymn to Christ as [to] a god' (*Epp.* 10.96). Writing at about the same time, Ignatius, bishop of Antioch, speaks of singing (in praise of) Jesus Christ, of singing (praise) 'in one voice through Jesus Christ to the Father' (*Eph.* 4.1–2), and of singing (praise) 'to the Father in Jesus Christ' (*Rom.* 2.2).

Of great interest is the possibility that the psalms sung by the first Christians were understood to be addressed to Christ.[32]

---

[30] See e.g. G. Vermes, *The Complete Dead Sea Scrolls in English* (London: Allen Lane/ Penguin, 1997) 243–332.

[31] See also 1 Cor. 14.26; Jas. 5.13.

[32] 'The influence of Psalm 110 and other psalms reflected in the New Testament is probably to be accounted for by positing their familiarity through wide and frequent

In particular, Hebrews 1.8–12 suggests that Psalms 45.6–7 and 102.25–27 may have been so understood, and Bauckham wonders if this was the type of hymn to which Ephesians 5.19 and Pliny's report refer.[33] On the other hand, the readiness to see Christ in or referred to in the Psalms may be better understood as evidence of hermeneutical more than liturgical practice. In fact the application of Psalms to Christ in Hebrews highlights the rich diversity of the christology involved. For example, we may recall Hebrews 1.6 using Psalm 97.7 as a summons to God's angels to worship his Son. Hebrews 1.8–9 cites Psalm 45.6–7, both addressing the Son as 'God' and as affirming that the Son's God has anointed him. Hebrews follows the widespread early Christian practice of referring Psalm 110.1 ('The Lord said to my Lord, "Sit at my right hand until I make your enemies a footstool under your feet"') to the exalted Christ (Heb. 1.13),[34] and then a few verses later also refers to Christ Psalm 8.4–6 (Christ as fulfilling God's purpose in creating humankind). And, as Martin Hengel notes, in Hebrews 2.12 the author seems to have understood Psalm 21.23 as referring to 'the exalted Son (intoning) the praise of the Father in the midst of the gathering of the redeemed congregation, his brethren'.[35] So, once again, the data is more complex and the implications not so clearly drawn.

---

usage in earliest Christian worship' (Hurtado, *Origins* 88–9). On this whole subject see particularly M. Hengel, 'Hymns and Christology', *Between Jesus and Paul* (London: SCM Press, 1983) 78–96; also 'The Song about Christ in Earliest Worship', *Studies in Early Christology* (Edinburgh: T&T Clark, 1995) 227–91. Both have been republished in German in M. Hengel, *Studien zur Christologie: Kleine Schriften IV* (WUNT 201; Tübingen: Mohr Siebeck, 2006) 185–204, 205–58. For fuller bibliography see Hurtado, *Origins* 86 n. 55, and *Lord Jesus Christ* 147 n. 161.

[33] Bauckham, *Jesus and the God of Israel* 137–8; see further M. Daly-Denton, 'Singing Hymns to Christ as to a God (cf. Pliny, *Ep.* X, 96)', in Newman, et al. (eds), *Jewish Roots* 277–92. Horbury notes the increasing acceptance 'that the Christ to whom hymns were sung as to a god in the reign of Trajan was already honoured in essentially the same way 70 years earlier among Galilean and Judean Christian Jews' (*Jewish Messianism* 116–17).

[34] See Ch. 4 n. 24.

[35] Hengel, 'Song' 237–8.

Also of considerable interest is the possibility that the New Testament contains some of the original hymns or canticles sung by the first Christians. The most obvious of these are the worship songs or poems included in Luke's birth narratives. Many congregations will be familiar with the Magnificat, the Song of Mary, and the Benedictus, the Song of Zechariah (Luke 1.46–55, 68–79). They have been sung in Christian churches for many centuries, perhaps even in the first generation or two of Christianity. They are canticles in praise of God, not Christ, though Christ (and John the Baptist) can be regarded as the occasion for the praise. The same is true of the Gloria – 'Glory to God in the highest' (Luke 2.14); and the Nunc Dimittis – 'Master, now let your servant depart in peace' (2.29–32).

More controversial (as hymns) are the poems or purple passages identified in the Pauline letters (though only in the twentieth century). The two most famous are Philippians 2.6–11 and Colossians 1.15–20. They have been prominent in all recent attempts to understand the earliest christologies of the New Testament and so should be quoted in full:

> Think this among yourselves, which you think in Christ Jesus
> (or, which was in Christ Jesus),
> who being in the form of God
>   did not count equality with God something to be grasped,
> but emptied himself,
>   taking the form of a slave,
>   becoming in the likeness of human beings.
> And being found in form as man,
>   he humbled himself
>   becoming obedient to death,
>   death on a cross.
> Wherefore God exalted him to the heights
>   and bestowed on him the name that is over every name,
> that at the name of Jesus every knee should bow . . .
> and every tongue confess that Jesus Christ is Lord,
>   to the glory of God the Father.
>
> (Phil. 2.5–11)

He is the image of the invisible God, the firstborn of all creation;
for in him were created all things in heaven and on earth
visible and invisible, whether thrones or dominions
or principalities or authorities;
all things were created through him and for him.
He is before all things,
and in him all things hold together.
And he is the head of the body the church.
He is the beginning, the firstborn from the dead,
in order that in all things he might be pre-eminent.
For in him God in all his fullness was pleased to dwell,
And through him to reconcile all things to him,
Making peace through the blood of his cross through him,
Whether things on earth or things in heaven.

(Col. 1.15–20)

Christ is clearly the subject of these hymns; they can properly be called 'Christ hymns'. What they are *not*, however, is hymns *to* Christ.[36] If they are hymns of the first Christians (the claim is disputed), they are hymns to God, praising God *for* Christ. The same is true of other passages that have been identified as early Christian hymns.[37] It is, of course, no surprise at all that what Christ has done, or what God has accomplished through Christ, was the subject of earliest Christian worship. Nor is it a surprise that Christ was the occasion of earliest Christian worship and that earliest Christianity inaugurated a whole new kind of hymnody. Furthermore, it can be argued that praise being offered *for* the exaltation of Jesus Christ as God's right-hand plenipotentiary would logically and naturally entail that praise be offered also *to* the plenipotentiary himself.[38] Even so

---

[36] Hengel lumps them all together as 'hymns to Christ' and concludes that 'the hymn to Christ grew out of the early services of the community after Easter, i.e. it is as old as the community itself' ('Hymns and Christology' 93); similarly Hurtado, *Lord Jesus Christ* 142. R. Deichgräber, *Gotteshymnus und Christushymnus in der frühen Christenheit* (Göttingen: Vandenhoeck & Ruprecht, 1967), draws his conclusions with greater circumspection (207–8).

[37] Notably John 1.1–18; 1 Tim. 3.16; Heb. 1.3; 1 Pet. 3.18–19, 22.

[38] Hengel points out that if Pliny had in view 'a song about Christ in which predicates of God were applied to Christ', this would be similar to the Johannine prologue (John 1.1–18) and the hymn in Phil. 2.6–11 ('Song' 263).

it is not clear when this step was taken and whether the hymns evident in the Pauline letters provide evidence that Pliny's description of early second-century Christian worship would have been appropriate 50 years earlier.

The only clear New Testament examples of hymns sung to Christ are the shouts of praise in the book of Revelation. There we find acclamations of God – typically:

> You are worthy, our Lord and God,
>   to receive glory and honour and power,
> for you created all things,
>   and by your will they existed and were created.
> (Rev. 4.11, NRSV)[39]

But as well as acclamations of God there are acclamations of the Lamb (Christ) – typically:

> Worthy is the Lamb that was slaughtered
> to receive power and wealth and wisdom and might
> and honour and glory and blessing!
> (Rev. 5.12; also 5.9–10, NRSV)

Furthermore, there are acclamations of God and of the Lamb together – typically:

> To the one seated on the throne and to the Lamb
> be blessing and honour and glory and might
> for ever and ever!
> (Rev. 5.13, NRSV)[40]

Whether these should all be classified as 'hymns' is an unnecessary quibble. What is clear, nonetheless, is that Christ was linked with God in hymns or shouts of praise that elsewhere are given only to God. And it is not hard, or pushing the data too far, to envisage the seer's language as reflecting the liturgical practice of his community.[41] Nor is it hard to imagine the Christians who were hauled in for questioning in Bithynia, probably only

---

[39] See also Rev. 4.8; 7.12; 11.17–18; 15.3–4; 16.7; 19.1–3, 5.
[40] Also 7.10; 11.15; 12.10–12; 19.6–8.
[41] Hengel, 'Hymns and Christology' 81–2; Hurtado, *Origins* 90.

a decade or two later, recalling such hymns and acclamations when they gave the testimony that Pliny described as their singing hymns to Christ as (to) a god.

2.3 Sacred space, sacred times, sacred meals, sacred people

Universally characteristic of worship is the dedication to the one worshipped of sacred places where the worship is to be offered, sacred times at which the worship is to be offered, sacred meals to celebrate formative events and traditions, and sacred people to ensure that the worship offered is acceptable to the one worshipped.

(a) Sacred space

There is no question that the sacred space, indeed *the* sacred space, for Israel was the Temple in Jerusalem. The holiness of the Temple was rooted in the awe-inspiring encounter between Moses and God at Mt Sinai (Exod. 19). The sanctity of that encounter carried over to the tent of meeting in which Moses continued to encounter God during Israel's wilderness wanderings (Exod. 34.29–35). This in turn carried over to the Temple itself built by Solomon, when the glory of the Lord filled the house of the Lord at its dedication (1 Kings 8.10–11). And although the Temple suffered much abuse and destruction, its theological and symbolical significance was always central to Israel's religion, a centrality and significance enhanced by the massive building work of the Herodian Temple, which stood in Jerusalem at the time of Jesus and the first Christians. That the Temple was a defining locus and identity marker for all Jews, the majority who were outside the holy land as well as those resident in Israel itself, is sufficiently indicated by the fact that all male Jews over 20, wherever they lived, were expected to pay the Temple tax of a half-shekel every year, and by the popularity of the three pilgrim festivals celebrated in Jerusalem at the Temple each year. In short, the Temple was understood to be the place where God had chosen to put his name, to be the focal point for the divine–human encounter in which the religion of Israel was rooted, and to be the means by which the covenant relationship between God and Israel was maintained.[42]

Jesus' attitude to the Temple is not entirely clear.[43] In taking part in Temple ritual and worship, as he must have done on visits to Jerusalem, he would have observed the purity laws by which the sanctity of the Temple was safeguarded. The famous episode known as 'the cleansing of the Temple' (Mark 11.15–17 pars.) is sometimes regarded as a critique of the Temple itself. By preventing the business transactions on which the offering of sacrifice depended, it is possible that Jesus was rejecting the practice of sacrifice as such. But it is more likely that the criticism implied in this action was a criticism of abuse; the Temple had become 'a den of robbers' (11.17). And the scripture that Jesus cited on that occasion ('My house shall be called a house of prayer for all nations' (Isa. 56.7)) would seem to indicate a hope for that function to be fulfilled, that the Temple would indeed fulfil its function as a house of prayer not only for Israel but 'for all nations'. Another possibility arises from the word about the Temple's destruction and rebuilding that Jesus must have uttered in one form or another (John 2.19). We know that the Qumran community regarded themselves (that is, their community) as in effect a replacement for the Temple. Perhaps the new or rebuilt Temple for which Jesus looked would consist of the community of his disciples. The fact that three of the central figures in the earliest Christian community were regarded as 'pillar' apostles (Gal. 2.9) suggests that they were thought of as pillars in the temple of God, as envisaged in Revelation 3.12.[44]

The attitude of the first Christians to the Jerusalem Temple is similarly unclear, or ambivalent. They evidently continued to attend the Temple to take part in the daily prayers (Acts 2.42, 46; 3.1). The conservative Jewish believers in Messiah Jesus,

---

[42] See e.g. E. P. Sanders, *Judaism: Practice and Belief 63 BCE – 66 CE* (London: SCM Press, 1992) 47–145; C. T. R. Hayward, *The Jewish Temple: A Non-biblical Sourcebook* (London: Routledge, 1996).

[43] See the discussion in my *Jesus Remembered* 636–40, 785–90, 795–6.

[44] See again *Jesus Remembered* 514–15; also *Beginning from Jerusalem* 210.

'zealots for the law', evidently regarded themselves as still bound to observe the Temple-focused rituals of the law (21.20, 23–24, 26). Yet we also read of Stephen, probably a leader of the 'Hellenists' (6.1–6), who seems to have taken up Jesus' warnings about the Temple (6.13–14), and who suffered summary execution as a result (7.58–60). The speech attributed to Stephen critiques the suggestion that God dwells in any house made by humans (7.48–50), and the description of the Temple as 'made with hands' amounts to regarding the Temple as idolatrous (cf. 7.41). For Stephen, to think of God as available through the Temple ritual was in effect to treat the Temple as an idol.[45]

This latter attitude to the Temple was the most common among the first Christians, apart from the conservative believing Jews. In his writings Paul ignores the Temple and characterizes the present Jerusalem as a kind of slavery (Gal. 4.24–25). Indeed, he transfers the image and theology of the Temple to describe the individual believer and the believing community: 'you [plural] are the temple of God and God's Spirit dwells in you'; 'your body is a temple of the Holy Spirit within you' (1 Cor. 3.16; 6.19). He still believed in the importance of purity, not the ritual purity without which one could not enter the Jerusalem Temple, but rather spiritual purity: circumcision in the flesh was unnecessary since they had been circumcised in their hearts by receiving the Spirit;[46] the laws concerning what was clean and unclean no longer applied (Rom. 14.14, 20); the necessary washing and purification had been accomplished by the Spirit and the word.[47] He rejoiced that Christians now had immediate access to the divine grace; that is, without having to go to, and receive it by means of, the Temple (Rom. 5.2). It could even be argued that Paul transferred the notion of sacred space to the market place. For he called on the Roman believers to present their *bodies* as a sacrifice (Rom. 12.1) – the point

---

[45] On the Hellenists and Stephen's attitude to the Temple see my *Beginning from Jerusalem* 246–73.

[46] Rom. 2.28–29; Phil. 3.3; Col. 2.11.

[47] 1 Cor. 6.11; 2 Cor. 7.1; Eph. 5.26.

being that the body is the means by which embodied beings communicate with one another (seeing with the eye, hearing with the ear, speaking with the mouth, etc.). So the call is for believers to offer themselves up in their corporeal relationships, their everyday relationships, with the same commitment and devotion that a priest would express in offering a sacrifice in the holy place.[48] It is in such dedicated living that one experiences the presence of God.

The letter to the Hebrews focuses on what appears to have been the continuing attractiveness of the Jerusalem Temple cult for some early believers. The main thrust of its exposition is even stronger than Paul's: that the Temple and its cult only foreshadowed the reality now experienced by believers (Heb. 10.1; but note Col. 2.17). The Temple, with its Holy Place and Holy of Holies, was only a mirror or symbol of heaven, where God really is. And now Christ has opened the way into the real Holy of Holies in heaven, that is into the very presence of God. Consequently the writer can exhort his readers and audiences, 'Let us approach the throne of grace with boldness' (4.16; 10.22), for it is no longer necessary to seek the divine presence and grace through the Jerusalem Temple. In fact the Jerusalem Temple is passé, its job now done, its ritual obsolete (chs 8—10).

With such theology, the understanding of the sacred space has been transformed. The place where God and humans can meet is no longer restricted to a physical holy place, or even understood as especially mediated through a sacred space. If the community is the Temple, or the individual believer's body indwelt by the Spirit is the Temple, then that is where God is to be encountered. The New Testament writers as a whole (as also Jesus) were intent on focusing on the reality of encounter with God, the reality of the gift of the Spirit, and re-evaluated the sacred space and sacred ritual of previous generations accordingly. Some did indeed maintain the importance of sacred space and traditional ritual, and they are represented in some measure in the New Testament. And Paul for one was anxious

---

[48] See further my *Theology of Paul* 543–5.

to respect the inhibitions of more conservative believers in clinging to their traditions (particularly Rom. 14.1—15.6). But it was the existential reality of divine presence rather than of sacred space that gave them their ground for worship and made their worship so empowering.

In consequence there is little reason to look for sacred spaces dedicated to Jesus within the New Testament, as though we might find a holy site consecrated to him, and where he was exclusively worshipped. Some attempts have been made to argue that the tomb of Jesus was such a place of worship for the earliest Christians. But of that we have no indication in the New Testament whatsoever. Acts gives no hint of it. And Paul, who operated in Jerusalem and returned to Jerusalem on several occasions, never implies that he visited the tomb where Jesus had been buried or attended worship there. The only locations mentioned in connection with earliest Christian worship in Jerusalem are the Temple (ironically) and the earliest believers' own homes. Not even the tomb where Jesus had been laid appears to have been reckoned as a sacred space by the first Christians.

What we do have, however, should not be disregarded. Above all we should remember that Paul speaks of the community of believers, of each church in various places, as *the body of Christ* in that place (1 Cor. 12; Rom. 12.4–5). We should also bear in mind his frequent phrase 'in Christ', which in many instances has a locative meaning.[49] It was belonging to Christ, being 'in Christ', being the body of Christ, that provided the Christian equivalent to the holy place. If the Jerusalem Temple was the key identity marker for Jews both in the land of Israel and in the Jewish diaspora, then Christ himself was the defining identity marker for the first Christians (Christ-ians). Christ himself functioned in effect as the Christian sacred space. That is not the same as a place dedicated to Christ. But it does imply that every Christian and Christian community is the sacred space

---

[49] Full details in *Theology of Paul* #15.2.

dedicated to Christ, through which others should be able to encounter Christ.

(b) Sacred times

The sacred times for Israel and, given their heritage, the first Christians were the Sabbath and the annual festivals. Observance of the Sabbath was a key expression of Israel's covenant responsibility before God,[50] and an essential feature of a proselyte's conversion to Judaism (Isa. 56.6). Indeed, the unusualness of such a regular day of rest (every seven days) not only marked out the distinctiveness of Judaism but also made Israel's religion very attractive to other nationalities.[51] In Jewish thought Sabbaths were regularly linked with 'new moons and feasts' as a way of speaking of the main festivals of Jewish religion.[52] The festivals in view were particularly Passover, Pentecost, the Day of Atonement and Tabernacles.

As with sacred space, so with sacred time, the first Christians were somewhat divided. Jesus was remembered as having debated with Pharisees over the observance of the Sabbath (Mark 2.23—3.5 pars.), but the issue seemed to be more a question of *how* the Sabbath should be observed, not *whether* the Sabbath should be observed. At the same time, Jesus seems to have honoured the pilgrim feasts, most notably the feast of the Passover during his final week in Jerusalem (Mark 14.12–25 pars.). Among the earliest Jerusalem believers, presumably the 'zealots for the law', were those who counted more traditional observance of the Sabbath as an expression of their loyalty to the law. Paul also refers to those who regarded some days as more important than others (Rom. 14.5–6). But in the same passage he also refers with sympathy, or at least without

---

[50] Exod. 20.8–11; 31.16–17; Deut. 5.15.

[51] Josephus can even say that 'there is not one city, Greek or barbarian, not a single nation, to which our custom of abstaining from work on the Sabbath day has not spread' (*Against Apion* 2.282).

[52] 1 Chron. 23.31; 2 Chron. 2.3; 31.3; Neh. 10.33; Isa. 1.13–14; Ezek. 45.17; Hos. 2.11; 1 Macc. 10.34; CD 3.14–15; 1QS 9.26–10.8.

disapproval, to Christians who did not regard any single day (the Sabbath would almost certainly be in mind) as more important than others. And he was critical of those in Colossae who made an issue of 'festivals, new moons or Sabbaths' (Col. 2.16). Yet the pilgrim feasts may have continued to provide significant dates for Paul (as suggested by Acts 20.16 and 1 Cor. 16.8), even if he now regarded Christ as the Passover lamb (1 Cor. 5.7).

More to the point, probably, are the indications that the first Christians were accustomed to meeting on 'the first day of the week' (Acts 20.7; 1 Cor. 16.2). Since this was the day of Jesus' resurrection (Mark 16.2 pars., where we find the same phrase), it may fairly be deduced that the first Christians met on that day every week to celebrate the resurrection of Jesus. Moreover, the seer of Revelation attests that his initial inspiration was received on 'the Lord's day' (Rev. 1.10). This became established as the Christian name for Sunday,[53] and Ignatius explicitly contrasts it with the Sabbath, as the day 'on which our life arose through him and his death' (*Magn.* 9.1). Thus, the Lord's day evidently became the pre-eminent Christian sacred time, the Sunday being seen as a weekly celebration of Easter. Easter itself was no doubt the equivalent annual celebration of Jesus' resurrection, with what became known as the Christian Good Friday and Easter taking over from the Jewish Passover.

We can speak quite properly, then, of the traditional Jewish sacred times both as transformed into different times (Sunday rather than Sabbath) and as having different commemorative and symbolical significance (Jesus' death and resurrection rather than Passover and exodus from Egypt). That the Sunday was 'the Lord's day', belonging to the Lord, dedicated to the Lord Jesus Christ, no doubt signifies that Christ was the content of the worship offered then, and presumably suggests that the worship was offered in his name or through him or to him.

---

[53] *Didache* 14.1; Ignatius, *Magnesians* 9.1; *Barnabas* 15.9; Justin, *Apology* 1.67.3–8; Eusebius, *Ecclesiastical History* 4.26.2.

(c) Sacred meals

Communal meals were a feature of most religions or cults, and of clubs or societies or voluntary associations at the time of Jesus and the first-generation Christians. The most obvious example within Judaism was again the Passover meal, commemorating the deliverance of Israel from slavery in Egypt. But shared meals were one of the most characteristic features and *raisons d'être* of voluntary associations and cults.[54] Indeed, clubs were sometimes described as *eranoi*, an *eranos* being a meal to which each contributed his share (what we might call a 'potluck' dinner). Such meals would regularly include ritual acts of devotion, sacrifice or libations to the patron god in whose temple premises the club met. Many portions of papyri have been discovered, for example, containing invitations to dine at the table of the Lord Sarapis.[55]

The sacred meal of the first Christians was 'the Lord's dinner/ supper' (1 Cor. 11.20–26), subsequently more usually referred to as the Eucharist. That it shared characteristics with other sacred meals of the time is obvious enough from 1 Corinthians 8 and 10. Paul made it clear that participation in other such meals for believers was impossible: 'you cannot partake of the table of the Lord and the table of demons' (10.21); that is, to partake of a meal in the temple of an idol, eating food sacrificed to idols, should not be considered acceptable among believers (8.10–11). The implication is that at the Lord's meal the Lord Christ was himself the host, just as Sarapis was conceived as the host of the meals to which he gave invitation, the body of Christ (10.16) taking the place of the meat that had come from the sacrifices made to Sarapis. Such parallels could well encourage the inference among onlookers that the Lord Christ was a god like Sarapis, and the one to whom the Christians offered their devotion.[56] The meal was not simply a commemoration of what

---

[54] More details in *Beginning from Jerusalem* 609–17.

[55] *Beginning from Jerusalem* 616 n. 78.

[56] So also Hurtado, *Origins* 85; Fee comments that 'there can be very little question that this is *the Christian version of a meal in honor of a deity*' (*Pauline Christology* 491–2 – his emphasis).

Jesus had done. It was much more a means of bonding the participants with the one whose meal it was, the one who was the heart of the meal as well as Lord of the meal. Clearly envisaged here is a devotion to Christ that at least is not far from worship.

(d) Sacred persons

Integral to all communal worship from times immemorial is recognition of the need for someone to mediate between God/ the god and his or her worshippers. This is pre-eminently the role of the priest. And to make it possible for the priest to fulfil that role it has always been recognized that the priest must be set apart in one degree or other for this special function. To mediate access to the sacred space, the priest must himself (almost always a 'him') be sanctified, rendered sacred/holy. So, in the religion of Israel, the priests alone were able to enter the Holy Place of the Temple, and the high priest alone was able to enter the Holy of Holies, the very presence of God himself, and then only on one day of the year, the Day of Atonement. And similar rites were followed in almost all religions of the ancient world.

It is of particular interest, then, that priests hardly feature in earliest Christianity. We can be more precise. According to Luke's account in Acts, many priests joined the new sect in the earliest days of the new movement (Acts 6.7). But there is no hint that they functioned among the believing congregations as priests. Instead we find the idea that believers as a whole are priests (Rev. 1.6; 5.10; 20.6), 'a holy priesthood', 'a royal priesthood, a holy nation' (1 Pet. 2.5, 9). Paul describes his own ministry in characteristically priestly terms (Rom. 15.16), but by doing so he probably was not thinking of himself as part of a distinct order of priesthood within the earliest Christian community. For it is his mission work, rather than his pastoral work, that he describes in these terms. And he uses such language elsewhere to refer to the responsibility of all Christians (to offer sacrifice) and to the kindly ministry of Epaphroditus in coming to his aid (Rom. 12.1; Phil. 2.25). Any and all ministry in or on behalf of the gospel could thus be described as priestly ministry.

The key point, presumably, was that the first Christians had no need of priests. They did not need anyone to mediate between them and God or the Lord Christ. They did not depend on any order to open the way into the sacred space of divine presence. The way had been opened by Christ for all to follow. No New Testament writing brings this out more forcefully than the letter to the Hebrews. For Hebrews, the belief that worship and approach to God require an order of priesthood is no longer valid. The order of Aaronic priesthood belongs to the past, to the time of foreshadowing (Heb. 7—8). The reality is now that only one priest is necessary – Christ himself, a priest according to the order of Melchizedek. No other can share that priesthood, since no other shares the qualification that only Christ has (Heb. 7.3). And no other need share that priesthood, since through the priesthood of Christ the way has been once for all opened to the Holy of Holies, the very presence of God himself. The argument of Hebrews began to be lost to sight in the second century, as the desire for Christianity to be recognized as a religion resulted in the re-emergence of the concept of a separate order of priests within the Christian community.[57] But for the first Christians, the existential experience of knowing God immediately, without any mediation other than that of Jesus, was too real and too precious to be quickly lost to sight.

2.4 Sacrifice

In the ancient world the most characteristic feature of worship was sacrifice, the offering of produce as a gift to the god or, more often, the sacrifice of an animal, its blood being regarded as a propitiation to avert the god's anger or an expiation to blot out the worshipper's sins. This was above all why there needed to be a sacred space, a space safeguarded from human pollution, so that a sacrifice acceptable to the god could be offered there. Today we would find horrendous the never-ending rivers of

---

[57] See further my *The Partings of the Ways between Christianity and Judaism* (London: SCM Press, 1991; [2]2006) #12.6.

blood that flowed from the altar(s) in most temples. This was where the meat for the meals in the temple dining rooms came from – the meat not used up in the sacrifice itself or given to the priests. Sacrifice and meal went together; those who ate the sacrifices were partners in the altar (1 Cor. 10.18). This was primarily why priests were necessary: priest and sacrifice went together; no priest, no acceptable sacrifice. It was this logic that shaped Christian thought from the second century onwards: since Christ's death was a sacrifice, there had to be both a priest to offer the sacrifice and an altar on which the sacrifice was offered.[58]

The point of relevance here is that sacrifice and deity also go together. Sacrifice was the supreme acknowledgment of the deity of the one to whom the sacrifice was offered. Sacrifice could be described as 'the ultimate criterion of deity'.[59] That was why the imperial cult was so significant as it spread west in the Roman Empire. For to offer a sacrifice to the Emperor was to affirm and acknowledge that the Emperor was (already) a god, though the Emperors during the first generation of Christianity usually resisted the emperor cult because of that implication. For the same reason Jews regarded the offering of sacrifices to idols as wholly unacceptable, since the practice was a public affirmation of the deity of pieces of stone and wood, and a god made by human hands was a contradiction in terms and an impossibility.

Within the religion of Israel sacrifice played a crucial role, but always as sacrifice to the God of Israel alone. Twice every day, morning and evening, in the Jerusalem Temple a male yearling lamb was offered to God as a burnt sacrifice, along with flour, oil and wine (Exod. 29.40). Regularly sacrificed by individuals were burnt offerings and peace offerings (Lev. 1.4;

---

[58] See again n. 57, above.

[59] North, 'Jesus and Worship' 200. McGrath agrees: 'sacrificial worship [was] *the* defining feature of Jewish exclusive devotion to only one God'; 'the sacrificial worship of the one God without images was the make-or-break issue' (*The Only True God* Ch. 2; here 31, 35).

3.1), and especially sin offerings and guilt offerings (Lev. 5).[60] These last two were the principal sacrifices, since they expiated sins and transgressions. As the letter to the Hebrews puts it, 'Without the shedding of blood there is no forgiveness of sins' (Heb. 9.22). The sin offering and the scapegoat were central to the annual Day of Atonement ritual, by which the sins of the people as a whole were dealt with (Lev. 16). There was never any thought that such sacrifice should be offered to anyone other than God. Sacrifices to any other gods were simply sacrifices to lifeless idols.

The earliest Christian attitude to Israel's sacrificial ritual is ambiguous. According to Matthew Jesus accepted the obligation to pay the Temple tax, which funded the daily morning and evening sacrifice (Matt. 17.24–27). But he also pronounced sins forgiven, without any reference to a priest or sin offering.[61] As already noted, Jesus' cleansing of the Temple and prophecy of its destruction could be interpreted as a rejection of the sacrificial ritual. But his talk of a renewal of the covenant (or of a new covenant) at the Last Supper (Mark 14.22–24 pars.) could also imply that he saw his imminent death as a covenant sacrifice, a sacrifice that sealed the covenant (Exod. 24.8).

Similarly ambiguous is the attitude of the first Christians. According to Luke, the first believers were constantly in the Temple,[62] and Peter and John went to the Temple at the hour of the evening sacrifice (Acts 3.1). Luke says that Paul himself participated in the Temple rituals (21.23–24, 26). At James' suggestion he joined with four men who were under a vow. He purified himself with them and paid their expenses, in order that they might shave their heads. The circumstances envisaged are presumably those covered by the legislation in Numbers 6.9–12, where a Nazirite's defilement required a seven-day purification, the shaving of the previously uncut hair, and on the

---

[60] For detail see Sanders, *Judaism* Ch. 7.

[61] Mark 2.5–7, 10; 3.28; Luke 7.47–49. Similarly John the Baptist? – *Jesus Remembered* 358–61.

[62] Luke 24.53; Acts 2.46; 5.42.

eighth day the offering of two turtle doves or young pigeons, the one as a sin offering, the other as a burnt offering in atonement for his sin.

In a passage of great importance, Paul recalls that the gospel faith that he inherited affirmed 'that Christ died for our sins in accordance with the scriptures' (1 Cor. 15.3). He received this confession presumably immediately after his conversion, which was probably within two years of Jesus' crucifixion. So this was one of the earliest Christian statements of faith. That Jesus' death was being thus regarded in terms of a sin offering, or as the equivalent of the scapegoat on the Day of Atonement, is confirmed by other Pauline passages.[63] From this it can be inferred that (many or most of) the first Christians regarded Jesus' death as sacrificial, a sacrifice that removed, expiated, cleansed from sin. The inference can be extended: to refer to Jesus' death as a sacrifice for sin was to imply that no other sacrifices for sin were thereafter necessary for those who believed in Jesus. This is the line that the letter to the Hebrews powerfully developed: the old sacrifices were ineffective; Christ's sacrifice was alone effective; that once-for-all sacrifice highlighted the old sacrifices' inadequacy and rendered them unnecessary (Heb. 10.1–18). 'Where there is forgiveness of (sins) there is no longer any offering for sin' (10.18). Perhaps the Hellenists, like Stephen, who distanced themselves from the Jerusalem Temple, were already drawing this conclusion, and it was they who framed the confession that Paul inherited.[64]

At the same time, we should note that the imagery to describe the efficaciousness of Christ's death 'for sin' was drawn from the sacrificial ritual of Israel. Indeed, we could say that *it could only be meaningful as imagery for Christ's death if the sacrificial ritual had been regarded as meaningful and effective.* This was the way Israel's sins had been dealt with for many centuries. So the use of sacrificial imagery to make theological sense

---

[63] Rom. 3.25; 8.3; 2 Cor. 5.21. See further *Theology of Paul* #9.2–3.
[64] See n. 45, above.

of the death of Jesus depended on the assumption that the sacrificial ritual of the sin offering itself made theological sense. Not only so, but presumably it was because bloody sacrifice was regarded generally in the ancient world as constitutive of religious worship that the first Christians should inevitably understand Jesus' death as a sacrifice.

This line of reflection takes us too far away from our main inquiry, so I will not pursue it further here. The point of relevance for us that emerges, however, is that in earliest Christianity, *Christ was never understood as the one to whom sacrifice was offered*, even when the imagery of sacrifice was used symbolically for Christian service.[65] Christ was generally understood as the sacrifice that dealt effectively with sin. Christ was less frequently understood as the priest who made the sacrifice, the exception being in the letter to the Hebrews, where Christ is both sacrificing High Priest and sacrificial victim! Even in the book of Revelation, Christ is 'the Lamb who had been slaughtered'. If then being offered sacrifice is 'the ultimate criterion of deity', Jesus would not seem to qualify. Yet at the same time we should recall that Paul saw the death of Jesus as an act of God: God put Christ forward as a sacrifice of atonement (Rom. 3.25); it is Christ's death that demonstrates the love of God (5.8). The logic seems to run counter to the rationale of sacrifice as offered to God. God was involved in the sacrifice itself and in the offering of the sacrifice, as well as the receiving of the sacrifice. So if God is on both sides of the transaction, presumably we should not press a strict subject–object antithesis in considering to whom the sacrifice of Christ was offered. Perhaps if God was on both sides of the sacrifice of Christ, so also Jesus was somehow on both sides – not as the one to whom sacrifice was offered in the death of Christ, but as bound up with the receiving of God just as much as God was bound up in the giving of Christ as sacrifice.

---

[65] North, 'Jesus and Worship' 199, referring to Rom. 12.1; Phil. 2.17; 4.18; Heb. 13.15–16; 1 Pet. 2.5.

2.5 Conclusion

It is important to recognize how distinctive the practice of earliest Christian worship was. Prayers were said and hymns sung; to that extent earliest Christian gatherings conformed to the regular practice of worship in other cults. Nevertheless, their gatherings for worship and for shared meals were unique. Unlike any other cult or club, there was no sacred space in which they met, no far-off Temple towards which they directed their worship. Their sacred time was different and distinct, their sacred meal allowed no comparison or competitor. There were no priests present to officiate and to render their meals acceptable or their worship possible. No sacrifices were offered; there were no libations to any god. Onlookers might well wonder whether this *was* a cult, whether their gatherings were religious, as the practice of religion was generally understood.

That Jesus was central to early Christian worship is not to be doubted. He was the reason why their prayers could be offered with confidence and the principal subject of their hymns. It was his name they invoked; they appealed to him in times of personal crisis. And their praise of God naturally included praise of Christ. He was himself the sacred space in whom they met as his bodily presence ('body of Christ') still on earth. It was his day on which they met most regularly. Their sacred meal was his supper, the key elements his body and blood. He alone was the priest through whom they could now come to God. His sacrificial death had dealt with their sins and opened the way to God. Their entry into the divine presence was possible not only *because of* what he had accomplished (Good Friday and Easter), but *through* him and in him.

An important corollary should not be missed. We can now see that our starting question, 'Did the first Christians worship Jesus?', is too narrow and may be misleading. And the answers that so far have emerged may be equally misleading: few prayers as such are recorded as being made to Jesus; few hymns are recorded as being sung to Jesus; no sacrifices were offered to him as to a god. But such findings have only partially answered the question, and have shown that the question thus posed is rather naïve, as though the issue was whether Jesus had somehow replaced a remote God, so that worship was now to be directed to him, perhaps even to him rather than to God. But what we have seen in this chapter is the earliest Christian conviction that Jesus was wholly bound up with their worship: that he was the one who had brought God near to them; that prayers were offered to God through him, and appeals made to him were not thought of as odd; that he was the content and worthy recipient of their praise; that the space and context of worship was given by him, in a real sense *was* him; that he was the food and drink of their worship, the means by which they came to God. So the question is not so much 'Did the first Christians worship Jesus?', but rather, 'Was earliest Christian worship possible without and apart from Jesus?' Was earliest Christian worship so closely bound up with Jesus that inevitably he participated in the receipt of worship just as he participated in the offering of the worship? Was earliest Christian worship in part directed to him as well as made possible and enabled by him?

This brings us to the next phase of our inquiry.

3

Monotheism, heavenly mediators and divine agents

So far we have focused on the term 'worship' in trying to answer our question, 'Did the first Christians worship Jesus?' Most of the evidence so far considered discourages an unequivocal 'Yes', and points at best to a qualified 'Yes', or perhaps more accurately a qualified No! Worship language was little used with reference to Jesus. Apart from the hymns of Revelation, the practice of worship rarely had Jesus (the Lamb) in view as the one worshipped. Yet it also became increasingly clear that to answer the question solely in these terms was to miss important aspects of the evidence. For again and again it became evident that the worship of the earliest Christians involved Jesus in different ways. Not only was he the theme and content of their worship – hardly surprising for Christians – but also Jesus was understood as bound up with their worship, as its locus and mediator. They worshipped *in* him and *through* him. Their entry into the very presence of God was possible not simply *because of* Jesus, by virtue of what he had done in the past in his mission, death and resurrection, but also *by means of* Jesus, by virtue of the continuing presence and ongoing role as the risen and exalted Christ. So a simple 'No' or 'Yes' (or more 'No' than 'Yes') in answer to our central question is simply inadequate.

Now therefore we will view the question from another perspective. Thus far we have examined the question of 'worship'. But now we need to focus on the one worshipped. If we are to use the term 'worship' in a tight or narrow way (only God/god is to be worshipped), then we have to ask how loose or wide is the word 'God'/'god'? We have clarified to some extent the term 'worship'. But now we have to clarify the term 'God'/'god', and the relation of Jesus to that term.

We begin by looking at how Israel would have focused and restricted its worship. Jesus' reply to the tempter, '(You shall) worship the Lord your God and (shall) serve only him' (Matt. 4.10/Luke 4.8) quoted Deut. 6.13.[1] That passage followed on from Deuteronomy 6.4, which became Israel's principal credo, the *Shema*: 'Hear O Israel: the Lord our God is one Lord', or 'the Lord our God, the Lord is one'. What did this 'oneness' mean? What did it mean to serve (*latreuein*) only him?

These questions invite a consideration of:

- what is usually described as Israel's 'monotheism';
- Israel's concept of angels, particularly 'the angel of the Lord' and the great angels;
- Israel's concepts of the divine Spirit, of Wisdom and of the Word;
- and the apotheosis (glorification or deification) of human beings.

As should be obvious, it is important to clarify how restricted was Israel's worship since that is the context within which our question, 'Did the first Christians worship Jesus?', arises. Our question may thus be reformulated: 'Given that Israel restricted its worship to God, the one God, did the first Christians include Jesus within this restricted worship, or did they somehow loosen the restrictions, or did they regard the restrictions as excluding Jesus and as in effect forbidding the worship of Jesus?'

I should at once acknowledge that this way of exploring how earliest high christology came to expression – that is by comparing and contrasting how Second Temple Judaism conceptualized the immanence of God, how God interacted with his creation and his people – has been a well trodden path for several decades. The material is usually grouped under the heading of 'divine agency' or 'heavenly intermediaries' or 'divine

---

[1] Deut. 6.13 does not say 'only' here, but the rendering of Matt. 4.10/Luke 4.8 is an acceptable compression of the fuller text – 'The Lord your God you shall fear; him you shall serve, and by his name alone you shall swear' – especially in the light of Deut. 6.4.

hypostases'.[2] Bauckham has expressed some reservation about such attempts 'to find a model for Christology in semi-divine intermediary figures in early Judaism' and regards such trends as 'largely mistaken'. He prefers to focus rather on 'the unique identity of the one God' in early Judaism and argues that 'from the earliest post-Easter beginnings of Christology onwards, early Christians included Jesus, precisely and unambiguously, within the unique identity of the one God of Israel'.[3] I will have to comment on this use of the term 'identity' later.[4] Here it is simply necessary to observe that Bauckham's attempt to distance his approach from the 'divine agency' approach is questionable. For he recognizes that to speak of God's Spirit, his Word or his Wisdom is to speak of God: these, he avers, 'are included in the unique identity of God'; 'as aspects of the unique divine identity, they are included in it'.[5] So it is not entirely clear why an attempt to clarify how such ways of speaking of God (of God's identity) is 'largely mistaken' as a way of clarifying how Jesus was included within that identity. Even the talk of angels cannot be excluded from such an attempt, since, as we shall see, the 'angel of the Lord' tradition within Israel's scriptures and early Judaism was also a way of speaking of divine presence. And even the question of apotheosis cannot be excluded from consideration, since the christological issue is precisely how a man, Jesus of Nazareth, could be said to embody/incarnate God. So, despite Bauckham's misgivings, a study of how early Judaism

---

[2] Early examples are G. H. Box, 'The Idea of Intermediation in Jewish Theology', *JQR* 23 (1932–3) 103–19; W. Bousset and H. Gressmann, *Die Religion des Judentums im spälhellenistischen Zeitalter* (HNT 22; Tübingen: Mohr Siebeck, 1925, [4]1966) Part 5. More recently see particularly my *Christology in the Making* (London: SCM Press, 1980, [2]1989; Grand Rapids: Eerdmans, 1996); L. W. Hurtado, *One God, One Lord: Early Christian Devotion and Ancient Jewish Monotheism* (Philadelphia: Fortress, 1988); A. Chester, *Messiah and Exaltation: Jewish Messianic and Visionary Traditions and New Testament Christology* (WUNT 207; Tübingen: Mohr Siebeck, 2007).

[3] Bauckham, *Jesus and the God of Israel* ix, 2–3.

[4] See further Ch. 4.7.

[5] Bauckham, *Jesus and the God of Israel* 16–17, 158–9, 182–5. If Second Temple Jews 'drew the line of distinction between the one God and all other reality clearly' (3), then Spirit, Wisdom and Word were understood to belong on the side of the one God.

(the matrix within which earliest high christology came to expression) conceptualized divine immanence and agency is necessary if a clear answer to our central question is to be attained.[6]

We start, however, by clarifying what is meant by Jewish 'monotheism'.

3.1 'The Lord our God is one Lord'

It has often been observed that in Deuteronomy the *Shema* (Deut. 6.4) should be understood in the same way as the first of the Ten Commandments: 'You shall have no other gods besides (or before) me' (Exod. 20.3). That is, it does not deny the existence of other gods, but calls for Israel's devotion to Yahweh to be exclusive.[7] Even when we read the earlier passages in Deuteronomy – 'the Lord is God; there is no other besides him' (4.35); 'the Lord is God in heaven above and on earth beneath; there is no other' (4.39) – that could be taken to mean that Yahweh is unique (as we might say, the only god who is God), and the only god for Israel.[8] This is better described as monolatry (the worship of only one god) rather than monotheism (the belief that there is only one god/God), or perhaps as 'henotheism' (belief in one's god without asserting that he or she is the only god).[9]

The issue is complicated by the fact that Yahweh had not been the only name used for Israel's god/God. We find several other names, such as El-Elyon (God Most High), Shaddai

---

[6] Cf. McGrath's critique of Bauckham for suggesting that the early Jews had a clarity of definition of 'divine identity and uniqueness' that is not borne out by their writings (*The Only True God* 12–15, 117 n. 3).

[7] Yahweh has become the regular way of writing the tetragrammaton; that is, the four-lettered name revealed to Moses in Exod. 3.14 – YHWH.

[8] R. W. L. Moberly, 'Towards an Interpretation of the Shema', in C. Seitz and K. Greene-McCreight (eds), *Theological Exegesis: Essays in Honor of Brevard S. Childs* (Grand Rapids: Eerdmans, 1999) 124–44; also 'How Appropriate is "Monotheism" as a Category for Biblical Interpretation?', in Stuckenbruck and North (eds), *Early Jewish and Christian Monotheism* 227–30.

[9] McGrath presses the point that in earliest Judaism 'many forms of acknowledgment of, and interaction with, figures understood to be subordinate to God Most High were considered compatible with Jewish monotheism' (*The Only True God* 30).

(Almighty) and Elohim (God) in the patriarchal narratives. Did these originally denote several gods worshipped by the patriarchs, or were they simply different titles for God who came to be known by Israel especially as Yahweh, or indeed were they actually titles of other gods absorbed by Yahweh? The fact that the Hebrew word Elohim is itself a plural form raises another question of some relevance to us: what is the oneness of a plurally denoted God? The plural form used in the first creation narrative, 'Let us make humankind in our image, according to our likeness' (Gen. 1.26), has long posed just such a tantalizing issue.

The most likely answer to the question of Israel's monotheism is that early Israel regarded its God as the supreme God, unique in relation to other beings designated as god, in a class of his own, as alone Creator, alone final Judge.[10] Above all, this God was the God of Israel, the God who had revealed himself to the patriarchs and to Moses, who had rescued Israel from bondage in Egypt, and who had made a covenant with Israel as his own people: 'I am the Lord your God, who brought you out of the land of Egypt, out of the house of slavery; you shall have no other gods before me' (Exod. 20.2). And this foundational belief grew into a conviction more aptly described as monotheism, of which the prophet Isaiah (or Second Isaiah) is the clearest exponent:

> There is no other god besides me,
> a righteous God and a Saviour;
> there is no one besides me.
>
> Turn to me and be saved,
> all the ends of the earth!
> For I am God, and there is no other.
>
> (Isa. 45.21–22, NRSV)

---

[10] See particularly R. Bauckham, 'Biblical Theology and the Problem of Monotheism', in C. Bartholomew, et al. (eds), *Out of Egypt: Biblical Theology and Biblical Interpretation* (Milton Keynes: Paternoster, 2004) 187–232 (here 210); reprinted in *Jesus and the God of Israel* 60–106 (here 86–7); see also 107–9. Note also L. W. Hurtado, 'First Century Jewish Monotheism', *JSNT* 71 (1998) 3–26, reprinted with small editorial changes in *How on Earth* 111–33.

Certainly the oneness of God, or the conviction that only Yahweh was worthy to be designated God and worshipped as God, is well established by the first century CE. As the Alexandrian Jewish philosopher Philo puts it early in the first century when commenting on the first commandment:

> Let us, then, engrave deep in our hearts this as the first and most sacred of commandments, to acknowledge and honour one God who is above all, and let the idea that gods are many never even reach the ears of the man whose rule of life is to seek for truth in purity and guilelessness (*De Decalogo* 65).[11]

Josephus, the Jewish historian, writing at the other end of the first century, makes the same point regarding the decalogue: 'the first word teaches that God is one'; recognition of the one God, he affirms, was common to all Hebrews (*Jewish Antiquities* 3.91; 5.112). As the great rabbinic scholar Ephraim Urbach notes, 'The belief common to all Jews at the beginning of the first century was that their God was the only God and their religion the only true religion.'[12]

From our point of view it does not matter whether the religion inherited by Jesus and his first Jewish disciples was technically monotheistic or monolatrous.[13] We may

---

[11] More examples in Bauckham, *Jesus and the God of Israel* 210 n. 67.

[12] E. E. Urbach, 'Self-Isolation or Self-Affirmation in Judaism in the First Three Centuries: Theory and Practice', in E. P. Sanders (ed.), *Jewish and Christian Self-Definition: Vol. Two. Aspects of Judaism in the Graeco–Roman Period* (London: SCM Press, 1981) 269–98 (here 273). See also S. S. Cohon, 'The Unity of God: A Study in Hellenistic and Rabbinic Theology', *HUCA* 26 (1955) 425–79, and P. Rainbow, 'Jewish Monotheism as the Matrix for New Testament Christology: A Review Article', *NovT* 33 (1991) 78–91, both summarized by Hurtado, *How on Earth* 117–20. Hurtado also notes the scruples expressed by faithful Jews about worship and prayer to figures other than God (121–9).

[13] M. Mach, 'Concepts of Jewish Monotheism during the Hellenistic Period', in Newman, et al. (eds), *Jewish Roots* 21–42, notes cases of both exclusive monotheism (2 Isa., Judith, *Sib. Or.* 3) and inclusive monotheism (*Jubilees*, 1QM). W. Horbury, 'Jewish and Christian Monotheism in the Herodian Age', in Stuckenbruck and North (eds), *Early Jewish and Christian Monotheism* 16–44, maintains that 'exclusive monotheism was not clearly the dominant tendency in the Herodian age. Rather, exclusive and inclusive types of monotheism were concurrent, and the inclusive type was also influential . . . The conditions of the Herodian age . . . were suited to

recall that Paul seems to share a similar ambivalence on the subject:

> Even though there may be so-called gods in heaven or on earth –
> as in fact there are many gods and many lords – yet for us there
> is one God, the Father . . .   (1 Cor. 8.5–6, NRSV)

What matters is that only one was worthy to be worshipped as God, the God of Israel. This conviction had been reinforced by Israel's long history of resisting the claims of other gods: for example, the syncretism with the Baal worship encouraged by King Ahab and his wife Jezebel (1 Kings 16.31–33), or the syncretism of the Syrian overlords in the second century BCE as they tried to persuade the Judeans that Yahweh was just another name, the local name, for Olympian Zeus.[14] As the speech attributed to Stephen, the first Christian martyr, reminded its listeners (Acts 7.42–43), the Babylonian exile was the consequence of Israel's entrancement with worship of the host of heaven.[15] We should equally recall the scathing attacks on pagan idolatry in Jewish literature, in which idols were scorned as nothing beside the living God of Israel.[16] It was the memory of Israel's own golden calf failure at Mt Sinai (Exod. 32), the memory of the chief cause of the Babylonian exile, and the memory of the Maccabees' nation-shaping resistance to the syncretistic hellenizing policy of the Syrian regional power in the 160s BCE, that made Israel's affirmation of the *Shema* and

---

interpretation of Jewish monotheism in ways that rigorous monotheists might have avoided, and did later seek to avoid' (43–4). The evidence has caused some scholars to question whether 'monotheism' is the most appropriate word to describe Israel's belief; e.g. J. F. A. Sawyer, 'Biblical Alternatives to Monotheism', *Theology* 87 (1984) 172–80; P. Hayman, 'Monotheism – a Misused Word in Jewish Studies?', *JJS* 42 (1991) 1–15. It is in view of such findings and misgivings that Bauckham has attempted to reformulate the issue in terms of the uniqueness attributed to Israel's God (n. 10, above).

[14] 1 Macc. 1.41–50; 2 Macc. 6.1–2.

[15] Amos 5.25–27; similarly Jer. 19.1–13.

[16] Especially Isa. 44.9–20; Wisd. 11–15; Ep. Jer.; *Sib. Or.* 2.8–45.

of the first commandment so strong and so emphatic at the time of Jesus.[17]

All that said, we need to remember also that the epithet 'god' could be used of kings and judges even within Israel's scriptures themselves.[18] According to Exodus, Moses was commissioned to 'serve as God' to Aaron (Exod. 4.16; 7.1), and Philo does not hesitate to interpret this as God 'appointed him as god'; Moses 'was named god and king of the whole nation'; Moses was 'no longer man but God'.[19] Similarly Josephus twice reports the speculation that Moses had been taken by or had returned to the deity.[20] Now of course this was not a departure from the monotheism or monolatry that Philo and Josephus clearly affirm elsewhere. What is interesting, however, is that given their monotheism/monolatry they nevertheless had no apparent difficulty in using such language hyperbolically or in symbolical terms. The implication is that however central and of crucial importance the *Shema* was for all devout Jews at the beginning of Christianity, that did not prevent them from using god-language metaphorically or with poetic flourish.

3.2 Angels

Angels are familiar figures in religious perception of God's dealings with his human creation. In both Hebrew (*ml'k*) and Greek (*angelos*) the primary meaning is 'messenger', and the words can be used of a human messenger serving as an envoy.[21]

---

[17] The prophets found it necessary to rebuke Israel regularly for idolatry; see e.g. B. A. Levine, 'Scripture's Account: Idolatry and Paganism', in J. Neusner, et al., *Torah Revealed, Torah Fulfilled: Scriptural Laws in Formative Judaism and Earliest Christianity* (New York: T&T Clark, 2008) 3–24 (here 12–17).

[18] Pss. 45.6; 82.6; cf. Exod. 21.6; 22.8; Isa. 9.6–7.

[19] *De Sacrificiis* 9; *De Vita Mosis* 1.158; *Quod Omnis Probus Liber sit* 43 – though Philo immediately adds, 'though, indeed, a god to men, not to different parts of nature, thus leaving to the Father of all the place of King and God of gods' (43).

[20] *Jewish Antiquities* 3.96–97; 4.326.

[21] E.g. Gen. 32.3, 6; Josh. 7.22; 1 Kings 19.2; 2 Kings 6.33; Isa. 14.32; Ezek. 23.40; Luke 7.24; 9.52.

The words are used also of prophets as messengers of God.[22] But in both cases the terms are used pre-eminently of a messenger of God, 'the angel of the Lord', or 'the angel of God', and the Greek term has given us the transliteration into English of 'angel'. Thus God sends an angel to communicate with prophets,[23] and an interpreter angel appears regularly in apocalyptic visions and as companion in heavenly journeys.[24]

One of the most fascinating features of several ancient stories is the appearance of what can be called *theophanic* angels; that is, angels who not only bring a message from God, but who represent God in personal terms, or who even may be said to embody God. Thus the angel of Yahweh appears and speaks to Hagar in Genesis 16.7–12. But the story continues:

> So she called the name of the LORD who spoke to her, 'You are a God of seeing'; for she said, 'Have I really seen God and remained alive after seeing him?'   (Gen. 16.13)

Similarly in the other version of the same story, the angel of God speaks in the first person as God (21.17–18). In Jacob's dream the angel of God says, 'I am the God of Bethel' (31.11–13). Likewise in the theophany at the burning bush, the one who appears to Moses is described both as 'the angel of the Lord' and as 'the God of Abraham, Isaac and Jacob' (Exod. 3.2–6). In the wilderness wanderings of the children of Israel the divine presence in the pillar of fire and of cloud is spoken of both as 'the angel of God' and as 'the Lord' (Exod. 14.19–20, 24). And in Judges 2.1 'the angel of the Lord' says, 'I brought you up from the land of Egypt . . . I will never break my covenant with you.'

Clearly in these cases it is impossible to distinguish between the angel of Yahweh and Yahweh himself; they are obviously one and the same person. Or at the very least we have to say

---

[22] 2 Chron. 36.15–16; Isa. 44.26; Ezek. 30.9. Mark 1.2 and Matt. 11.10/Luke 7.27 all refer Mal. 3.1 ('I am sending my messenger ahead of you, who will prepare your way') to John the Baptist.

[23] E.g. 1 Kings 13.18; 19.5, 7; 2 Kings 1.3, 15; Zech. 1.9.

[24] As in Dan. 9.21–22; *1 Enoch* 19.1; 72.1; *4 Ezra* 2.44–48; 10.28–59.

that the narrators of these stories neither saw any need to make a clear distinction nor thought it important to do so. The point that emerges presumably is that the tellers of these stories were primarily intent to indicate the reality of the divine presence in these theophanic experiences. It is not that they wished to deny either the otherness of Yahweh, or that God was invisible to human sight. For this was an equally ancient perception and lay at the root of Israel's hostility to idolatry – the conviction that God is invisible, or, more precisely, *un-image-(in)able* (Exod. 20.4) and unlookable-on (Exod. 33.20).[25] Perhaps we should say they were abandoning the simplicities of an anthropomorphism that could speak of God as such appearing to human sight (as in Gen. 2—3). But a more sophisticated way of putting it would be to say that by speaking thus of the angel of the Lord they had found a way of denoting the reality of divine presence in such theophanic encounters without diminishing the holy otherness of Yahweh. The angel of the Lord in such stories was *a way of speaking of God's immanence without detracting from his transcendence*. The angel of God both was God and was not God. Alternatively expressed, the angel of God was God's way of manifesting himself to his servants without manifesting himself. The angel of God was not God as such but could be said to be God in his self-revelation.

In Israel's subsequent thought the subject becomes ever more complex.[26] For in what appears to be a burgeoning angelology we hear of high angels, or archangels. These angels stand in especially close relation to God, 'the angels of the presence'.[27] Four are most prominent – Michael, Gabriel, Raphael and the variously named Sariel/Uriel/Phanuel.[28] Here again we probably still have to say with Gerhard von Rad that 'the angels of Judaistic angelology are always a naïve representation of the

---

[25] See also e.g. Deut. 4.12; Sir. 43.31; Philo, *Post.* 168–69; Josephus, *Jewish War* 7.346.

[26] Mach notes that 'exalted angels and the like were – at least quite often – introduced when Jewish identity underwent a certain crisis' ('Concepts of Jewish Monotheism' 42).

[27] *Jub.* 1.27, 29; 2.2; etc.; *Test. Levi* 3.5; *Test. Jud.* 25.2; 1QH 6.13.

[28] Dan. 8.16; 9.21; 10.13; Tobit 12.15; *1 Enoch* 9.1–2; 20.1–8; 40; 1QM 9.15; 4QSl 37–40; *4 Ezra* 5.20.

omnipresent and omniscient word and will of Yahweh'.[29] A motivating factor in the growth of such an angelology will almost certainly have been the desire to depict Yahweh with the imagery of an all-powerful king who commanded a powerful army and whose majesty was attested by his extensive and glorious court retinue, as in the depiction of the heavenly counsel in Job 1.6 and 2.1.

Still more intriguing are the instances in the visionary and apocalyptic literature of later Israelite religion and of early Judaism; that is, up into the first century CE. In his awe-inspiring vision of the chariot throne of God, Ezekiel saw seated above the likeness of a throne the 'likeness as it were of a human form', with the appearance of a body of 'gleaming bronze' and enclosed round about by fire (Ezek. 1.24–27). This 'vision of God' became the basis for and stimulus to Jewish mysticism (Merkabah or chariot throne mysticism). What is also interesting, however, is that a few chapters later an angel appears to Ezekiel, who also had 'the appearance of a man', and whose torso was 'like gleaming bronze' and his loins of fire (Ezek. 8.2). Daniel too sees a similar glorious figure, loins 'girded with gold' of Uphaz, arms and legs like the gleam of 'burnished bronze' (Dan. 10.5–6). In the *Apocalypse of Zephaniah* (written some time during the first century BCE or first century CE) 'a great angel' appears, 'his face shining like the rays of the sun in its glory' and 'his feet like bronze which is melted in a fire' (*Apoc. Zeph.* 6.11–12). And the great angel in the *Apocalypse of Abraham* (first or second century) is identified as Yahoel (*Apoc. Ab.* 10.3). The name was almost certainly intended as a combination of Yahweh and El, and in obvious allusion to Exodus 23.21: 'Behold, I send an angel before you . . .; my name is in him.'[30]

Christopher Rowland has studied such texts closely and concludes that what he calls a process of 'bifurcation' was taking place in the perception of divine presence that these texts express. By this he means a process whereby the divine

---

[29] *TDNT* 1.81.

[30] See also Bauckham, *Jesus and the God of Israel* 225–7; 'the angel in question is the heavenly high priest' (225).

human-like figure on the throne in Ezekiel 1.26–28 seems to have become separated from the throne and to function separately as 'the agent of the divine will', with 'a gradual splitting in the way the divine functions are described'.[31] Rowland has put his finger on an important aspect of these heavenly visions, though I am less persuaded by the interpretation he offers and its appropriateness. The language used in such cases is that of the visionary, overwhelmed by the majesty of a heavenly figure seen in his vision. Such visions quickly drain the pool of imagery and language available to describe them. The heavenly glory that appears on such occasions to humans is by its nature overwhelming and blinding. What the language describes is the overpowering experience of such glory, while the precise identity of the glorious figure is not the primary concern. Here again it is a matter of seeing what is possible for human eyes to see, not of achieving a definitive description – a sense of being given the awesome privilege of seeing into the divine presence without clearly perceiving the manifestation of the deity or being able to distinguish the messenger of the deity from the deity as such.[32]

In fact, such visionaries and writers of apocalypses make a point of warning against the confusion that can so easily result from such glorious visions. The *Apocalypse of Abraham*, for example, insists that 'God cannot be looked upon himself' (*Apoc. Ab.* 16.3–4). And characteristically the glorious angel makes a point of forbidding the visionary to worship him. Thus the *Apocalypse of Zephaniah* 6.15 reads: 'He [the angel] said to me, "Take heed. Do not worship me. I am not the Lord Almighty, but I am the great angel, Eremiel . . ."' And in the *Apocalypse of Abraham* 17 'the angel knelt down with me [the apocalyptist] and worshipped' (17.2), and together they recite a hymn of adoration. This is all the more significant, since an angel who

---

[31] C. Rowland, *The Open Heaven: A Study in Apocalyptic Judaism and Early Christianity* (London: SPCK, 1982) 96–7, 100.

[32] Bauckham responds similarly to Rowland (*Jesus and the God of Israel* 160–1); see also Hurtado, *One God One Lord* 85–90.

bears Yahweh's name (Yahoel) could be said to share in at least some sense in Yahweh's identity![33]

Angels in the religion of Israel and early Judaism, therefore, are a reminder to us that in talk of worshipping God, the term 'God' can be just as unclear as the term 'worship'. Given the fundamental gap between Creator and creation, recognition of which was shared by most religions of the time, communication across that gap was problematic from both sides. It is Israel's conviction, of course, that God had communicated across that gap – to patriarchs, to Moses and to the prophets in particular. But human reception of that communication, and human perception of how that communication was achieved, were bound to be inadequate for the task, and bound to struggle to express how it came about. The concept of angels was one of the chief ways of perceiving that communication. But the very fact that predominant terms are not simply 'angels' but 'angels of the Lord', 'angels of God', and 'angels of the presence', is a reminder that already in Israel and in early Judaism the understanding was not simply of *communications* from God but of making real the *presence* of God.[34] The angel of the Lord was not simply an envoy from God and did not simply bring humans into the divine presence; rather he brought the divine presence into humans' daily reality – not simply a message from Yahweh, but the presence of Yahweh. He did not bring the whole of God (that was never possible), but he brought the real presence of God nonetheless.

---

[33] See also Tobit 12.16–20; *Joseph and Asenath* 15.11–12; and further Hurtado, *One God One Lord* 30–5; L. T. Stuckenbruck, *Angel Veneration and Christology* (WUNT 2.70; Tübingen: Mohr Siebeck, 1995); also 'Worship and Monotheism in the *Ascension of Isaiah*', in Newman, et al. (eds), *Jewish Roots* 70–89; also '"Angels" and "God"', where he notes cases of language of prayer and praise directed towards angels within a monotheistic framework, while also noting the difficulty of making sharp distinctions between 'veneration', 'worship' and 'cultic devotion'. The only one other than God who is properly worshipped in Second Temple Jewish literature is the mysterious Son of Man figure (of Dan. 7.14), as elaborated in the *Parables of Enoch* (*1 Enoch* 48.5; 62.6–9); the Son of Man is thought by some to be an angelic figure. Bauckham regards him as 'the exception that proves the rule' (*Jesus and the God of Israel* 171).

[34] 'The incorporation of angels into their view of God's sovereignty was apparently seen by devout Jews as compatible with their monotheistic commitment' (Hurtado, *Lord Jesus Christ* 34).

3.3 Spirit, Wisdom and Word

In Israel's theology angels were not the only heavenly intermediaries between God and humanity. Angels were sufficiently
distinct from God that the question of worshipping even great
angels, when it arose, was quickly dismissed. But the writers
of Israel's scriptures and of the post-biblical Jewish literature
(apocrypha and pseudepigrapha) had other ways of conceptualizing God's interaction with creation and divine immanence.
The most prominent of these were the Spirit of God, the
Wisdom of God and the Word of God.

(a) The Spirit of God

Although we find some overlap between angels and spirit(s)
in Jewish thinking, the Spirit of God was more naturally understood as closely identified with God, as a dimension or an aspect
of God, or as a way of characterizing God's presence and
power. For example, in 1 Samuel King Saul's state can equally
well be described as 'the Spirit of the Lord departed from Saul'
(1 Sam. 16.14) and as 'the Lord had departed from Saul' (18.12).
Since the Hebrew *ruach* has a range of meaning from 'wind'
to 'breath' and 'spirit', the wind at Israel's crossing of the Red
Sea can be called poetically the blast (*ruach*) of God's nostrils.[35]
'The Spirit of God' is synonymous with 'the breath of the
Almighty'.[36] In Isaiah 31.3 the power of *ruach* is the distinguishing characteristic of God, just as the weakness of flesh is the
characteristic of human beings. In Isaiah 'my Spirit', 'the Spirit
of the Lord' and 'God's holy spirit' are variant ways of speaking
of the divine presence, the divine 'I'.[37] Particularly in Ezekiel
'the Spirit' is synonymous with 'the hand of the Lord'.[38] And in
Psalm 139.7 'your Spirit' is set in synonymous parallel with
'your presence'. It is hardly surprising, then, that Paul can think

---

[35] Exod. 15.8; 2 Sam. 22.16. The vigorous metaphor is taken up by other writers – Job
4.9; Ps. 18.15; Isa. 30.27–28; 40.7; Wisd. 11.20.
[36] Job 33.4; 34.14; Ps. 33.6.
[37] Isa. 30.1; 40.13; 63.9–14.
[38] Ezek. 3.14; 8.1–3; 37.1.

of the Spirit of God as analogous to the human spirit: 'the Spirit searches everything, even the depths of God. For what human being knows what is truly human except the human spirit that is within?' (1 Cor. 2.10–11). As one could speak of one's spirit as one's inner being, a dimension or aspect rather than a part of oneself, so one presumably spoke of the Spirit of God as one of the ways of conceptualizing how God interacted with his creation and his people. The Spirit of God was/is the real presence of God, God breathing out his inspiration into prophet and sage.

Some would argue that in the literature of Second Temple Judaism the Spirit of God came to be treated as a semi-independent divine agent. Talk of the Spirit of God filling the world or being sent from on high, as in Wisdom 1.7 and 9.17, could be so interpreted. But a reading more consistent with the understanding of God in Israel and in early Judaism would think simply in terms of God's omnipresence and of divine anointing or inspiration. Similarly with the Spirit's role in creation, as in Judith 16.14 or *2 Baruch* 21.4, what Israelite or early Jew would read such passages as asserting a power other than the creative power of God at work? Are such passages any different from, for example, Psalm 104.30 ('When you send forth your Spirit they are created'), Psalm 143.10 ('Let your good Spirit lead me on a level path') or Isaiah 63.10 ('But they rebelled and grieved his Holy Spirit')? These are all simply ways of speaking about God, the outreaching creative action of God, the inspiration supplied by God, the innermost grief experienced by God at the behaviour of his people.

We can see from all this that from earliest times Israel's theologians recognized that there was what we might call a double aspect to God – on the one hand God invisible, unsee-able, un-image-(in)able, and on the other God acting upon creation and reaching out to humankind, in revelation, salvation and inspiration. The one aspect was what could never be experienced by humans or seen by human eyes (however close apocalyptic vision and mystic ecstasy came to that impossible ideal). The other aspect was God in his self-revelation, in and through creation, in inspiration and in redemption – not so much the Spirit of God as though the Spirit were a being different and distinct from God, but more accurately *God as Spirit.*[39]

Notably, *what we do not find is any hint that worship was offered to the Spirit of God.* Neither in the language of worship nor in the practice of worship do we find it thought to be appropriate that the Spirit should be seen as the one worshipped or to be worshipped. If the Spirit was seen as semi-independent of God, then such worship might have been thought to be appropriate. But the fact that no such worship or the question of the propriety of such worship seems to have entered the minds of Israel's prophets and sages, confirms that the Spirit was not seen as semi-independent of God. Rather we have to envisage an understanding of the reality of God as at least as complex as the reality of the human being. Perhaps, in view of the subsequent Christian Trinitarian understanding of God, we should be prepared to speak of a binitarian understanding of God in the religion of Israel and early Judaism.[40] But if so, what that amounts to is an understanding of God as both unknowable in his transcendence and knowable in his immanence.

(b) The Wisdom of God

The need for wisdom to lead a good and honourable life, a life pleasing to God, was fully recognized in the ancient religions. In Israelite religion, as elsewhere, a whole genre of wisdom literature became the most natural and fruitful means of

---

[39] See further M. Fatehi, *The Spirit's Relation to the Risen Lord in Paul* (WUNT 2.128; Tübingen: Mohr Siebeck, 2000) Part II: 'in Judaism as a whole the Spirit refers to God in his active role of relating to his creation and his people . . . the Spirit is never conceived of or experienced as an entity distinct or somehow separable from God. The Jewish experience of the Spirit is *always* and *essentially* an experience of God himself . . . the Spirit-language is used precisely when God's own personal presence and activity . . . is in view' (163).

[40] Hurtado is not persuaded that a postexilic Jewish binitarianism can be demonstrated (*One God One Lord* 37); the decisive 'mutation' to binitarianism does not take place till earliest Christian devotion to Jesus, which, however, was itself 'a direct outgrowth from, and indeed a variety of, the ancient Jewish tradition' (99).

exploring, explaining and exhorting the pursuit of wisdom. Jesus himself was a considerable teacher of wisdom, and in the New Testament the letter of James is a classic expression of wisdom literature.

Within Israel's wisdom literature it became common to speak of wisdom in personal terms, notably in Proverbs 1—9, where Wisdom is regularly portrayed as an attractive and persuasive woman in contrast to the corrupting female deities who offered themselves as prostitutes to draw individuals away from the Lord.[41] In the wisdom literature this figure of Wisdom is drawn in ever more elaborate and cosmic colours, as the wisdom by which God created the world, the wisdom at the heart of the universe. So in Proverbs 8.22–31 lady Wisdom claims to have been created at or as the beginning of creation, and to have been a companion with God in his creative acts, 'like a master worker (or little child)' (8.22, 30).

In the Wisdom of Jesus ben Sira (Ecclesiasticus) Wisdom sings a great hymn in praise of herself:

> Wisdom praises herself,
>> and tells of her glory in the midst of her people . . . :
> 'I came forth from the mouth of the Most High,
>> and covered the earth like a mist.
> I dwelt in the highest heavens,
>> and my throne was in a pillar of cloud.
> Alone I compassed the vault of heaven
>> and traversed the depths of the abyss . . .'
>> (Sir. 24.1–5, NRSV)

Similarly in the Wisdom of Solomon. She is described as 'the fashioner of all things' (Wisd. 7.22; 8.5–6). 'She reaches mightily from one end of the earth to the other and she orders all things well' (8.1). She 'sits besides God's throne' (9.4). And she is described at length as:

---

[41] Prov. 1—6 was probably counteracting the influence of the cult of the Mesopotamian goddess of love, Ishtar–Astarte, the 'strange woman' warned against in Prov. 2, 5, 6 and 7. See particularly R. N. Whybray, *Wisdom in Proverbs* (London: SCM Press, 1965) 87–92.

> ... intelligent, holy,
> unique, manifold, subtle,
> mobile ...
> For Wisdom is more mobile than any motion;
> because of her pureness she pervades and penetrates all things.
> For she is a breath of the power of God,
> and a pure emanation of the glory of the Almighty.
>
> (7.22–25, NRSV)[42]

Now, how should we understand such language? Some would argue, as in the case of the Spirit of God, that Wisdom was being portrayed as a divine being, an independent deity, like the near parallels in Egyptian and Mesopotamian religions. Or, alternatively that Wisdom was being seen as a semi-independent being, somewhat in the way that Jesus came to be seen as the second person or hypostasis in the Godhead.[43] But it makes much greater sense to see the language used of Wisdom as poetical or metaphorical. Three considerations point clearly in this direction.

First, Hebrew poetry delights in such personifications. For example, Psalm 85.10–11 depicts 'righteousness' and 'peace' as kissing each other.[44] Isaiah 51.9 calls upon the arm of the Lord to 'awake, put on strength'. In the novelistic love story of *Joseph and Asenath*, 'Repentance' is portrayed as 'the Most High's daughter ... the guardian of all virgins ... a virgin, very beau-

---

[42] In both Sir. 24.4 and Wisd. 11, the divine presence with Israel during the wilderness period is Wisdom.

[43] The term 'hypostatization' is regularly used to describe such depictions of Wisdom (e.g. Bousset and Gressmann, *Die Religion des Judentums* Ch. 18; other bibliography in my *Christology* 325 n. 21); Bauckham speaks of 'real hypostatization' (*Jesus and the God of Israel* 159). The concept of 'hypostatization' was an attempt to avoid a straight choice between Wisdom as an independent divine being and Wisdom as a personification. But the use of 'hypostasis' in this way is anachronistic, since that meaning for 'hypostasis' only emerged in the fourth century CE as part of an attempt to define God as Trinity; its use in this context in the first century would simply have been confusing. To use it for the period before Christianity is to claim, in effect, that the Christian Trinitarian conception of God had been anticipated in the Jewish Wisdom tradition.

[44] Paul similarly personifies 'righteousness' in Rom. 6.15–19 and 10.6.

tiful and pure and chaste and gentle' (15.7–8).[45] What Israel's
Wisdom writers seem to have been doing, then, is simply developing the technique of portraying desirable aspects of divine–
human relations by means of personification, by means of
elaborate metaphor. So in ben Sira the poetic analogies extend
to Wisdom being likened to a variety of beneficial trees
(24.13–17), and Proverbs' portrayal of divine wisdom as a
female figure is pressed into new modes of expression.

Second, it is hardly likely that the Wisdom writers were saying
something different from their more formal declarations, such as:

> The LORD by wisdom founded the earth;
> by understanding he established the heavens . . .
>
> (Prov. 3.19, NRSV)

> O God of my fathers and Lord of mercy,
> who has made all things by your word,
> and by your wisdom has formed man.
>
> (Wisd. 9.1–2)

Evidently then the hymns in praise of Wisdom are simply more
hyperbolic ways of praising God for the wisdom he displayed
in creating the world. Moreover, in both ben Sira and the
Wisdom of Solomon the distinction between Wisdom and Spirit
is very slight; like the Spirit, Wisdom is the breath of God.[46]
So both are a mode of speaking of God acting in a way that is
perceptible to the human mind. To say that God created the
world by Wisdom, is to say that God created the world wisely,
and that this wisdom is both evident to those with perception
and attainable for those who seek it.

Third, both ben Sira and the similar passage in the book of
Baruch (Bar. 3.9–37) end their eulogy of Wisdom by identifying
the Wisdom thus praised with the Torah:

> All this is the book of the covenant of the Most High God,
> the law that Moses commanded us
> as an inheritance for the congregation of Jacob.
>
> (Sir. 24.23, NRSV)

---

[45] Hurtado, *One God One Lord* 47–8.
[46] Sir. 24.3; Wisd. 7.25.

She is the book of the commandments of God,
  the law that endures for ever.
All who hold her fast will live,
  and those who forsake her will die.

(Bar. 4.1–2, NRSV)

Here clearly we see an apologetic or evangelistic motive at work. Since all morally responsible people desire wisdom, the Jewish sage both praised wisdom but also pointed to where, in Israel's experience, such wisdom is most to be found – in the Torah, the law of Moses. Here again we can hardly speak of personal beings distinct from God, but only of God's wisdom as it was embodied in the Torah.

Perhaps most significant of all, we know of no cult of Wisdom within Israel.[47] In the polytheistic religions surrounding Israel it would have been quite natural to set up such a cult and to offer sacrifices to Wisdom. But Israel praised Wisdom precisely to avoid and prevent its people being enticed to worship other gods. There was no thought of an Israel cult of Wisdom to outbid the attractiveness of Astarte or the other gods of their neighbours. Wisdom was praised in order to bind Israel more firmly to Yahweh. It was *the wisdom of God* that was being praised; *God in his wisdom*. And that wisdom was most clearly evident to Israel in the covenant God had made with Israel and in the law he had given to Israel.

So here again we have to recognize that the Israelite conception of God was not painted in monochrome. Israel's theologians did not insist that the only way to envisage God's interaction with his creation and with his people was by confessionally affirming his oneness. They were adventurous and liberal (or liberating) in their poetic and metaphorical God-talk. Their understanding of how God acted gave rise to imagery and symbols that at times may seem grotesque, but that together expressed the diverse reality of Israel's experience of God's acting on his people's behalf. To miss this point is to mistake their conception of God, of the one God, and to treat their

---

[47] The point is stressed by Hurtado, *Origins* 72–4.

conception of God in a narrow and stifling manner. Bauckham also weakens his argument by turning his back on attempts to illuminate earliest christology through the Jewish tradition of divine agency, and by in effect lumping the Jewish conceptualization of Wisdom under the heading of 'semi-divine intermediary beings'. This despite the fact that he fully recognizes that Wisdom (and Word) share the divine identity.[48] If he and I are right, Wisdom was *not* regarded as a 'semi-divine intermediary', but was a way of speaking of God's activity in creation and salvation. The issue we have to leave open at this stage is whether 'divine identity' captures adequately or most effectively the thinking behind these early Jewish attempts to speak of God's immanence without calling his transcendence into question.

(c) The Word of God

That God acts by speaking and communicates by speech is taken for granted in Israel's tradition. The scriptures common to Judaism and to Christianity begin with a dramatic sequence of divine commands – 'Then God said, "Let there be light"' . . . 'And God said, "Let the waters bring forth swarms of living creatures"' . . . 'Then God said, "Let us make humankind in our image"' – in describing the successive acts of creation by which God brought form and life to formless and lifeless matter.[49] The phrase 'the word of the Lord' occurs more than 240 times in the Hebrew scriptures, and the great bulk of these (over 90 per cent) describe a word of inspired prophecy. Thus again and again we read, 'the word of the Lord came' to Abram, to Joshua, to Nathan, to Solomon, to Isaiah, to Jeremiah, to Ezekiel, to Hosea, and so on.[50]

In some cases the language used could suggest that the word is an entity in itself, something that comes from God, but assumes a life of its own. Thus there can be talk of God establishing his word (1 Kings 2.4); the Psalmist praises God's word (Ps. 56.4, 10), he trusts in God's word (119.42) and hopes

---

[48] As in *Jesus and the God of Israel* 217.

[49] Gen. 1.3, 6, 9, 14, 20, 24, 26.

[50] Gen. 15.1; Josh. 8.27; 2 Sam. 7.4; 1 Kings 6.11; Isa. 38.4; Jer. 1.4; Ezek. 1.3 (the phrase occurs nearly 30 times in Jeremiah and nearly 50 times in Ezekiel); Hos. 1.1.

in God's word (119.74, 81, 114); Isaiah speaks of the Lord sending a word against Jacob (Isa. 9.8) and affirms that 'the word of God will stand for ever' (40.8). But it is fairly obvious that these are just differing ways of speaking about what God has said through his servants.

The usage is still more extravagant in a number of cases. For example:

> By the word of the LORD the heavens were made,
>   and all their host by the breath of his mouth.
>
> (Ps. 33.6, NRSV)

> He sent forth his word and healed them.
>
> (Ps. 107.20)

> He sends forth his command to the earth; his word runs swiftly
> . . . He sends forth his word, and the ice is melted; he makes the
> wind blow, and the waters flow.   (Ps. 147.15, 18)

> For as the rain and the snow come down from heaven, and
> return not thither but water the earth, making it blossom and
> bear fruit, giving seed to the sower and bread to the eater, so
> shall it be with the word that goes forth from my mouth; it shall
> not return to me empty, but it shall accomplish that which
> I purpose, and prosper in the task for which I sent it.
>
> (Isa. 55.10–11)

More striking still is a passage in the Wisdom of Solomon, where the writer's customary focus on divine wisdom is supplemented by his description of the last of the ten plagues in Egypt, with a powerful image of the divine word:

> For while gentle silence enveloped all things,
> and night in its swift course was now half gone,
> your all-powerful word leapt from heaven, from the royal throne,
> into the midst of the land that was doomed,
> a stern warrior
> carrying the sharp sword of your authentic command,
> and stood and filled all things with death,
> and touched heaven while standing on the earth.
>
> (Wisd. 18.14–16, NRSV)

In all these cases the most natural way to read each of the passages is as a poetic flourish to heighten the significance and drama of what is being described. Today we are more aware that a spoken or written word can quickly assume a life of its own, as media reports and reviews take it in different directions, often well beyond (and even contradictory to) what the original speaker or writer intended. That is hardly to attribute a semi-independent or hypostatic status to the word itself. It is simply a natural, almost inevitable manner of speech, an obvious way of describing the effect and effectiveness of something said or written. In theological terms, it is the effectiveness of what God has said, that his word acts upon those addressed and brings about what God wills, which explains why the word of God can be spoken of in such terms.

The issue re-emerges with the Alexandrian Jewish philosopher Philo.[51] For the word, Logos (*logos*), is a major feature, or actor, and appears very frequently in Philo's numerous expositions of the Pentateuch. In many cases Philo speaks of the Logos as though he/it were a real being distinct from God, acting as an intermediary between God and the world. Thus the Logos is described as God's 'chief messenger, highest in age and honour', who 'pleads with the immortal as suppliant for afflicted mortality and acts as ambassador of the ruler to the subject' (*Quis Rerum Divinarum Heres Sit* 2–5). The Logos is 'the ruler and steersman of all' (*De Cherubim* 36). He/it is God's 'firstborn son, who shall take upon him its government like some viceroy of a great king' (*De Agricultura* 51), 'who holds the eldership among the angels, their ruler as it were' (*De Confusione Linguarum* 146). The Logos can even be described as 'the second God' (*Quaestiones et Solutiones in Genesin* 2.62).

However, it would be unwise to read such passages outside the context of Philo's world-view. For Philo's thought was heavily influenced by both Platonism and the Stoic thought of the time. The Platonic conceptualization of reality presupposes a basic distinction between the material world known to the

---

[51] For a fuller analysis see *Christology* 220–30, on which I draw in what follows.

senses and the world of eternal realities that can only be known by the mind. The implication of Platonic thought is that the contents of the material world are at best shadows and copies of the ideal or perfect forms of the heavenly world. The possibility of merging this cosmology with the Jewish way of looking at the relationship between this world and the heavenly was enhanced by the word to Moses: 'See that you make them [the furniture of the tabernacle] after the pattern for them, which is shown to you on the mountain' (Exod. 25.40). And from Stoicism came the concept of divine reason (*logos*) immanent in the world, permeating all things and present also in human beings – the 'seed logos' (*logos spermatikos*). The Stoic ideal was to live life in accordance with this divine reason.

Philo takes up both concepts. The Logos provides the transition from the heavenly world of ideal reality to the material world of the senses. A key is the realization that *logos* can mean both the unuttered thought and the uttered word by which the thought comes to expression. So, for example, Philo can interpret the passages mentioned above, where Moses is said to function as God to Aaron (Exod. 4.16; 7.1), in terms of Moses representing the unspoken thought or mind of God, while Aaron represents the spoken word of God.[52] Again, in his fullest treatment of the act of creation, Philo likens God's creative activity to that of the architect of a city who first plans the city in his mind and then constructs the city itself in accordance with the image, the blueprint in his mind (*De Opificio Mundi* 16–44). On this analogy the Logos is the reasoning faculty of God in the act of creating the universe. Alternatively expressed, the Logos is the archetypal idea, the overall plan that comes to material expression in creation.[53] It is only an alternative to or elaboration of this conceptuality that speaks of the Logos in terms of divine agency, as the power by which God effects his

---

[52] Philo, *Det.* 39–40, 126–32; *Migr.* 76–84; *Mut.* 208.
[53] *Opif.* 146; *Plant.* 18, 20; *Decal.* 134; *Spec. Leg.* 1.81, 171; 3.207; *Praem.* 163. See also McGrath, *The Only True God* 56–8.

creation, the unspoken idea coming to expression in the uttered creation-forming word.

Equally important for Philo was that the Logos is the intermediary between God and humankind. The invisible world, the heavenly world of ideal reality, is not accessible to the senses but only to the mind, the logos within answering to the divine Logos. To know this world of the mind, the real world, the divine Logos, was for Philo the goal of philosophy.[54] But beyond the intelligible world, beyond the Logos, is God himself, unknowable even to the purest intellect.[55] It is true that creation is a kind of shadow cast by God, and that one can discern the artificer to some extent by his works. And since God is the archetype of the Logos, to perceive the Logos is to perceive God in still fuller measure. But the Logos is as close as one can attain to God (*De Fuga et Inventione* 101). To come to the Logos is to realize that God in himself is still far beyond.[56]

In other words, for Philo the Logos is the mind or intention of God coming to expression in creation and in prophetic word. The Logos is God in his self-manifestation in creation, in inspiration and in salvation. The Logos is what is knowable of God, God insofar as he may be apprehended and experienced. 'That same word, by which he [God] made the universe is that by which he draws the perfect man from things earthly to himself' (*De Sacrificiis Abelis et Caini* 8). It is this mediating role of the Logos that Philo attempted to explain by the kaleidoscope of imagery we noted earlier. For Philo the Logos was a way of speaking about God while realizing that all attempts at such speech were bound to be inadequate. He did not and never would have thought of the Logos as somehow independent of God, far less as a divine being worthy of worship apart from God. His whole conceptuality of the Logos was an extension of Israel's more traditional poetic and metaphorical speech

---

[54] See e.g. *Opif.* 31; *Post.* 69; *Gig.* 60–61; *Migr.* 52; *Congr.* 79.

[55] Cf. *Leg. All.* 1.36–37; *Post.* 15, 168–69; *Immut.* 62; *Mut.* 9; *Praem.* 40, 44; *Legat.* 6; *Qu. Ex.* 2.67.

[56] See particularly *Som.* 1.65–66, 68–69; *Post.* 16–20.

about God's action and inspiration, made possible by the Platonic and Stoic world-view that he shared with so many of his intellectual contemporaries. Philo shows us just how widely a philosophical mind of the time could range in its attempt to speak with any degree of adequacy about knowing God and about God's revelatory action in relation to his creation and to humankind, and to do so without calling into question Israel's and early Judaism's firm monotheism. The Logos was the one God in his self-revelation. The thought of worshipping the Logos as a divine being other than God would never have entered Philo's head.

3.4 Exalted human beings

There is one other category that we should not ignore. It might at first seem to stand at some remove from what we have examined thus far. But in talking about the worship of Jesus we are (also) talking about the worship of the man Jesus of Nazareth. So we need to be alert to the fact that the concept of a human person being divinized was not unfamiliar in the world of Jesus' time. Legendary figures of the past in ancient myths were spoken of as having become gods; Heracles was probably the best known.[57] And the idea that the Emperor became a god when he departed this life was already common, even where the western Empire resisted the idea that the living Emperor was already divine. Such beliefs, of course, were quite far removed from the stricter monotheism of Israel and early Judaism. But there were still some potential precedents within Second Temple Judaism for understanding a particular individual to have been exalted or translated to heaven. The question is whether there was a precedent for the worship of such a person.

The key persons are the great figures of Israel's beginnings, particularly those cases where there was no knowledge of their burial (Moses) or where they were reported to have been taken

---

[57] *OCD*[3] 384–5.

to heaven without dying (Enoch and Elijah).[58] These cases are worth at least a brief review.

(a) Moses

We have already noted that the Jewish historian Josephus reported some speculation as to whether Moses had been taken or had returned to the deity (*Jewish Antiquities* 3.96–97; 4.326). More striking is 'The *Exagōgē*' of Ezekiel the Tragedian, written some time in the second century BCE, perhaps in Alexandria. In the *Exagōgē* Ezekiel describes a dream that was seen by Moses and interpreted by his father-in-law:

> On Sinai's peak I saw what seemed a throne
> so great in size it touched the clouds of heaven.
> Upon it sat a man of noble mien,
> becrowned, and with a sceptre in one hand
> while with the other he did beckon me.
> I made approach and stood before the throne.
> He handed o'er the sceptre and he bade
> me mount the throne, and gave to me the crown;
> then he himself withdrew from off the throne. ·
>
> . . .
>
> Then at my feet a multitude of stars
> fell down, and I their number reckoned up.
>
> (*Exagōgē* 68–80)
>
> . . .

Moses' father-in-law interprets the dream as predicting that Moses would cause a mighty throne to arise and that he himself would rule and govern men (85–86).[59]

What is striking about the poem is that it clearly draws on Ezekiel's vision of God on his chariot throne in Ezekiel 1 ('a man of noble mien'), and that it depicts Moses as replacing God on the throne. This of course could be understood as extravagant poetic hyperbole, drawing perhaps on the Genesis tradition of Joseph's dreams (Gen. 37.5–9). And in what seems to have followed in the *Exagōgē*, the poem reverts to describing

---

[58] See also Hurtado, *One God, One Lord* Ch. 3.
[59] I use the version by R. G. Robertson in *OTP* 2.811–12.

Moses in his traditional role and character as expressed in the narratives of Exodus.[60] So, although there is no thought of Moses being worshipped, nevertheless, and even allowing for the *Exagōgē*'s poetic extravagance, it remains striking that within a Jewish document from more than a century before the birth of Jesus Moses could be so depicted – in a similar role, it would appear, to that attributed to the man-like figure ('one like a son of man') who came to share Yahweh's Lordship in Daniel 7. Similar glorification of the memory of Moses we find in the so-called 'Moses Romance' of the Jewish Hellenistic historian Artapanus (second or first century BCE), where Moses is said to have been deemed worthy to be honoured like a god.[61]

(b) Elijah

Whereas it was unknown where Moses was buried (Deut. 34.6) – hence the scope for speculation as to what had happened to him – with Elijah there was no doubt. The story in 2 Kings 2 was clear: he had been taken up to heaven while still alive; that is, it would appear, without experiencing death. It was this conviction that Elijah had been translated to heaven without dying that led to the belief that he was holding himself ready to return to earth at the time of God's choosing. Thus the famous ending to the prophecy of Malachi:

> Lo, I will send you the prophet Elijah before the great and terrible day of the LORD comes. He will turn the hearts of parents to their children and the hearts of children to their parents, so that I will not come and strike the land with a curse.
>
> (Mal. 4.5–6, NRSV)

The thought and hope is taken up and its continuing attractiveness over the following generations is clearly reflected in ben Sira 48.9–10 and in the expectation reflected in the Gospels.[62]

---

[60] Ben Sira had already spoken of Moses being made 'equal in glory to the holy ones' in describing his mission and character (Sir. 45.2).

[61] *Fragment* 3.6 in *OTP* 2.899. See also D. M. Beegle, 'Moses', *ABD* 4.909–918 (here 916–17).

[62] Mark 6.15 par.; 8.28 pars.; 9.11–12 par.; 15.35–36 pars.; John 1.21.

Nor should we forget that in the Gospels' accounts of Jesus' transfiguration, the two who appear to Jesus, presumably also clothed in heavenly glory, were Moses and Elijah (Mark 9.2–8 pars.).

Again we should stress that there is no thought of Elijah being worshipped in any of these accounts. But again the precedent for the belief that Jesus had been exalted to share in heavenly glory should not be ignored.

(c) Enoch

Enoch is the earliest of the three great figures mentioned in this section, but the speculation and belief that came to focus on him makes it appropriate to consider him last. The point is that the same thing as happened to Elijah had apparently already happened to the ancient patriarch Enoch, the father of Methuselah: 'Enoch walked with God; then he was no more, because God took him' (Gen. 5.24). In other words, so Genesis was interpreted, Enoch had been translated to heaven without seeing death. Consequently he became a subject of considerable speculation, including his role as the heavenly scribe keeping note of human evil and writing condemnation and judgment,[63] and the possibility that he would return with Elijah.[64] The fascination with the figure of Enoch is evident particularly in the Enoch literature, now mostly contained in the book of *1 Enoch*. His translation to heaven is described in terms of a heavenly journey, in the course of which he is transformed into angel-like form,[65] and is identified as the Son of Man (of Dan. 7's vision) in the *Similitudes of Enoch* (*1 Enoch* 71.14). More strikingly, in *3 Enoch* (though it may be no older than the fifth or sixth century CE), Enoch (having been taken up to heaven) is identified as Metatron, the Prince of the Presence (3—16), even being called 'the lesser Yahweh' (12.5).[66] The feature here of particular interest to us is that this

---

[63] *Jub.* 4.17–19, 23; *1 Enoch* 12.4.

[64] *1 Enoch* 90.31; *Apoc. Elij.* 3.90–99. This speculation may be reflected in Rev. 11.3, the 'two witnesses' being Enoch and Elijah.

[65] *Asc. Isa.* 9.9; cf. *Jub.* 4.23; *1 Enoch* 71.11; *2 Enoch* 22.8.

[66] Probably with reference again to Exod. 23.21, 'For my name is in him'.

exaltation of Enoch as Metatron evidently came to be judged a threat to Judaism's monotheism; the heresy of calling Metatron a second 'divine power in heaven' was traced back to Elisha ben Abuya (*c.* 110–35 CE).[67] The data here relates to periods well after the first generation of Christians, but, as we shall see below, the sensitivities evident in the 'two powers heresy' may have been triggered in part at least by the early Christians' devotion to Christ.

We should not assume that these three figures (Moses, Elijah and Enoch) were exceptional in the degree of hagiography by which their memory benefited in the period of our concern (early to mid first century CE). We may note, for example, that in the Jewish apocryphal (that is, near biblical) literature, Jeremiah appears in 2 Maccabees 15.13–14 as a figure of heavenly majesty, and in the Wisdom of Solomon the righteous after death are numbered among the sons of God and their lot is with the holy ones, that is the angels (5.5). In the Dead Sea Scrolls Melchizedek (presumably with Gen. 14 in mind) is envisaged in the role, it would appear, of captain of the heavenly hosts (11QMelch. 2.9–11), and so possibly as exalted to angelic status, to function like or as one of the archangels.[68] Somewhat like Enoch and Elijah, in *4 Ezra* 14.9 Ezra is said to have been 'taken up from among men' to live in heaven 'until the times are ended'. In the *Testament of Abraham* 11 (Recension A), Adam is seen in heavenly glory on a throne. And probably most striking for us is the *Life of Adam and Eve* where we are told that the reason the devil was expelled from heaven was that he refused to worship Adam; that is, he refused to accept that he should worship the image of God (13–15).[69]

---

[67] *3 Enoch* 16; *b. Hag.* 15a. See A. F. Segal, *Two Powers in Heaven: Early Rabbinic Reports about Christianity and Gnosticism* (Leiden: Brill, 1977); D. Boyarin, *Border Lines: The Partition of Judaeo–Christianity* (Philadelphia: University of Pennsylvania Press, 2004).

[68] See further A. Aschim, 'Melchizedek and Jesus: *11QMelchizedek* and the Epistle to the Hebrews', in Newman, et al. (eds), *Jewish Roots* 133–5; Bauckham, *Jesus and the God of Israel* 221–4.

[69] Heb. 1.6 may have a similar thought in mind when it quotes Deut. 32.43, calling for all the *elohim* (gods/angels) to worship God, as a call to the angels to worship God's firstborn Son.

Nor should we forget 2 Peter 1.4, which speaks of the divine intention that believers 'may become participants in the divine nature'. *Theōsis*, 'deification', of humans is made much of in Orthodox Christianity, and has a much more substantial role in Christian theology than is usually recognized in the West.[70] No doubt this can be attributed to the influence of Greek thought, particularly the Platonic idea that there is a spiritual part of humanity that really belongs to the heavenly world and that can recover its true, godlike nature. Such influence is evident already in Second Temple Jewish literature.[71] So it is hardly surprising to find it in the New Testament, even though 2 Peter 1.4 is an isolated example.

All of this raises the possibility that even within the monotheistic Judaism of the first century the thought of a great human figure being exalted to heavenly status, and thus receiving the honour due to such a one, was not so far from being admissible. That the figures reviewed above were all ancient, legendary or even mythical figures weakens significantly any potential parallel. Nevertheless, the fact that even such a possibility was entertained within early Judaism remains significant. As angels, Wisdom and Word diminished or even bridged the infinite gulf between God and humankind from God's side, so, it may be said, the high evaluation placed on certain historic figures in Israel's history diminished the gulf from the human side. And the broader prospect of martyrs or virtuous persons being deified presumably diminishes the gulf still more.

3.5 Conclusion

How does all this help us to answer our question whether the first Christians worshipped Jesus? In different ways:

---

[70] See particularly S. Finlan and V. Kharlamov (eds), *Theōsis: Deification in Christian Theology* (Eugene: Pickwick, 2006).

[71] E.g. 4 Macc. 18.3; Pseudo-Phocylides 103–4; Philo, *Qu. Exod.* 2.29. See more fully R. J. Bauckham, *Jude, 2 Peter* (WBC 50; Waco: Word, 1983) 179–81.

- Israel's monotheism may leave the existence of other gods unclear, even if it asserts the uniqueness of Yahweh's deity. And it would appear that the 'oneness' of Second Temple Judaism's monotheism cannot simply be defined in terms of a numerical oneness. Confession of the *Shema* evidently did not discourage Israel's poets and theologians from using god-language metaphorically or with poetic flourish.
- The angel of the Lord and the various great angels of prophet and visionary were not simply envoys from God and did not simply bring humans into the divine presence; rather they brought the divine presence into humans' daily reality – not simply a message from Yahweh, but the real presence of Yahweh.
- Even more so, the Spirit, divine Wisdom, and the Logos were variously used as ways of speaking of God's immanence without infringing on his transcendent otherness. They enabled sages and philosophers to do what would otherwise have been impossible – to speak of the actual interaction of God with his creation and with his people.
- From the human side of the infinite gulf between God and humankind various apocalyptists and Hellenistic Jews were willing to speak of human beings having been exalted to near divine status.

In no case was the thought of worshipping other than God entertained. Or, to be more precise, when the thought did arise (worshipping a great angel?) it was quickly squashed. We can see, then, that for all that Second Temple Judaism had already created an atmosphere in which the question of Jesus being worshipped could arise, and arise as a natural corollary to the status attributed to him, it had provided no precedent to which the first Christians could appeal.

So, to answer our central question, we must now turn to the evidence of the New Testament itself.

4

The Lord Jesus Christ

In the first part of this brief study we examined the language and practice of the worship of the first Christians as attested by and reflected in the New Testament. The most consistent answer to the question, 'Did the first Christians worship Jesus?', was that Jesus was not usually worshipped as such, even though his name was regularly invoked in liturgical contexts, and even though he was linked with the Father in benedictions and his help was sought in particular personal crises. Except in the Apocalypse of John (Revelation), Jesus was the theme of hymns rather than the one to whom hymns were sung. There was no thought of sacrifice being offered to Jesus, only of Jesus as the decisive sacrifice making right the relationship between God and believers. Even so, it also became evident that a simple or predominantly negative answer to our question ('Did they worship Jesus?) did not provide an adequate assessment of all the New Testament data. For Jesus was not simply the object of praise, nor was what he had done only the reason for prayer. He was also understood to be the means by which those who believed in him could come to God: his body giving them their corporate identity; his body and blood giving them their spiritual nourishment; approach to the divine presence being in his name; he himself being the one through whom they could pray and draw near to God.

If the first part of our inquiry has focused on the *how* and *what* of worship, the second part has focused on the *whom* of worship. To whom is worship to be given? And if worship defines the one worshipped as god/God, who is to be defined as god/God alone worthy to be worshipped? In this second part of our inquiry we have started by examining the question of who was worshipped in Israel and in early Judaism. The answer in one sense was simple – only the God of Israel is to be worshipped. But here again the answer is not straightforward. For the ways in which God has made himself and his will known to Israel have been various, or so the scriptures of Israel and the sharpest minds of early Judaism attest. The one God – or should we say the only God? – had made himself known through angels – or should we say in angelic form? – and through his Spirit, by his Wisdom and in his Word – or should we say *as* Spirit, *as* Wisdom and *as* Word?

If God so encountered humankind in such ways, did that also determine the channels and focus of worship of the one God? If God comes to us in/as Spirit/Wisdom/Word, do believers come to him similarly through Spirit/Wisdom/Word? And if so, what corollaries follow for worship – not only for the *how* and *what* of worship, but for the *whom* as well? These are the kind of questions posed by our examination thus far and remain in mind as we turn to the testimony of the New Testament writers to ask whether Jesus was included in the who of the worship offered by the first Christians. The discussion naturally falls into several sections, and with an important corollary:

- Was Jesus a monotheist? Did he himself restrict worship to the one God?
- Jesus as Lord: the significance of Jesus' exaltation to heaven.
- Jesus as embodying the Wisdom of God, as incarnation of the Word of God and as the life-giving Spirit.
- Worship of the Lamb in Revelation.
- Jesus as god/God?
- The last Adam, mediator, heavenly intercessor.

Here again we remain in close dialogue with Hurtado and Bauckham. As already noted, Bauckham believes an approach to the New Testament data through or in the light of the material documented in Chapter 3 to be unhelpful or even mistaken; he prefers to approach the subject in terms of 'divine identity'.[1] But since Wisdom, Word and Spirit are almost

---

[1] See further introduction to Ch. 3.

certainly ways of speaking about God, about God's immanence and interaction with his cosmos and his people – which means they certainly share in God's identity – the possibility that such ways of speaking about God also informed the early Christian way of speaking about Jesus should surely not be ignored. Hurtado's argument takes seriously the earlier ways of speaking about God, but sees in the emergence of Christ devotion a decisive 'mutation' of this trend within Second Temple Judaism, a mutation without precedent. He refers to this as the 'binitarian shape' of earliest Christian worship, a 'characteristic "two-ishness" of their devotional practice', 'a distinctive pattern of binitarian devotion in which Christ is included with God as a recipient of devotion that can properly be understood as worship' within 'a strongly monotheistic religious commitment'.[2]

4.1 Was Jesus a monotheist?

The question, 'Was Jesus a monotheist?', has a slightly shocking ring for those brought up in the Christian tradition. It conjures up fanciful pictures of Jesus engaged in the great debates of the fourth and fifth centuries on God as Trinity, and the possibility of his refusing to affirm the Nicene Creed, or even siding with Jews and Muslims of later centuries in accusing Christians of tri-theism. But after the initial jolt, the appropriateness of the question in reference to a first-century Jesus soon asserts itself.

The relevance of the question should also be noted. Whether Jesus himself would have approved of the worship subsequently given to him is a question almost impossible to answer clearly and finally.[3] But it is one that should not be ignored, and an

---

[2] Hurtado, *One God, One Lord* 2–3; also *Origins* 63, 70–2.

[3] Hurtado does 'not think it necessary for Jesus to have thought and spoken of himself in the same terms that his followers thought and spoke of him in the decades subsequent to his crucifixion in order for the convictions of these followers to be treated as valid by Christians today', though he also notes that most Christians probably think that there was 'some degree of continuity' between what Jesus thought of himself and subsequent christology (*Lord Jesus Christ* 9). Later he rightly draws attention to 'the impact of Jesus' ministry and its consequences' (53–4; but also 60).

answer in terms solely of the high christologies of the Evangelists themselves, while entirely relevant, is in itself insufficient.

The question can be posed legitimately and meaningfully to the extent of asking whether Jesus would have shared the common beliefs of his fellow Jews of the time and would have affirmed that 'the Lord our God is one Lord' (Deut. 6.4). And if we can further inquire into Jesus' teaching in reference to God and draw legitimate inferences in this connection from the Jesus tradition, we will be well on the way to answering the question, to the extent that an answer is possible at this distance in time.

I offer first some inferences from Jesus' upbringing, then examine the explicit God-talk of his teaching as attested in the Jesus tradition, and finally probe what further deductions may be drawn from the impression he left on his disciples by the character of his mission.[4]

(a) Inferences from Jesus' upbringing

We can probably infer that Jesus was brought up by pious parents. Their piety is indicated by the names they gave their children (Mark 6.3) – James/Jacob (the patriarch), Joses/Joseph, Judas/Judah, Simon/Simeon – the latter three being the names of three of Jacob's 12 children, and heads of the resultant tribes. Nor need we hesitate to draw a similar inference from the name given to Jesus himself – Jesus/Joshua. Other inferences are worth noting briefly:

- A pious upbringing would include the tradition of reciting the *Shema* regularly. And the same inferences can be drawn regarding a practice of daily prayer, twice a day (Josephus, *Jewish Antiquities* 4.212) or even three times a day (*m. Ber.* 4.1).[5] As Joachim Jeremias observes, 'It is hardly conceivable

---

[4] In what follows I draw on my essay, 'Was Jesus a Monotheist? A Contribution to the Discussion of Christian Monotheism', in Stuckenbruck and North (eds), *Early Jewish and Christian Monotheism* 104–19.

[5] J. Jeremias, *The Prayers of Jesus* (London: SCM Press, 1967) 66–81; Sanders, *Judaism* 196–7, 202–8.

that the earliest community would have observed the hours of prayer had Jesus rejected them.[6]

- Likewise, we can probably assume that Jesus was brought up to attend the local synagogue Sabbath by Sabbath. The references to 'synagogues' in the Jesus tradition[7] and to Jesus' regular practice of teaching/preaching in Galilean 'synagogues'[8] should be sufficient to confirm both that such assemblies were an established feature of Galilean village life and that Jesus was a regular participant in such assemblies from childhood.
- The references to the 'tassels' of Jesus' garment[9] strengthen the impression that he himself was a pious Jew who took his religious obligations seriously.[10]
- At least some pilgrimage to Jerusalem for the great feasts can be assumed. Luke can even report that Jesus' parents 'went to Jerusalem every year at the feast of the Passover' (Luke 2.41). At any rate, we can assume that Jesus would have been familiar with the Temple and its functionaries, priests who served locally as teachers and magistrates (Mark 1.44 pars.), and the requirements of tithing (Matt. 23.23/Luke 11.42) and purity.[11]

Most of this is circumstantial, but the overall picture that emerges is certainly coherent and is entirely consistent with the affirmation of Jesus' belief and practice as a devout Jew. That this included the conviction and regular affirmation that 'God is one' is a corollary hard to escape.

---

[6] *New Testament Theology, Vol. 1: The Proclamation of Jesus* (London: SCM Press, 1971) 186–91 (here 188), referring to Acts 3.1; 10.3, 30; *Didache* 8.3.

[7] Mark 12.39 pars.; Luke 11.43; Mark 13.9/Matt. 10.17.

[8] Matt. 4.23/Mark 1.39/Luke 4.44; Matt. 9.35; Matt. 13.54/Mark 6.2/Luke 4.16; Luke 4.15; Luke 6.6; 13.10; John 6.59.

[9] Matt. 9.20/Luke 8.44; Mark 6.56/Matt. 14.36.

[10] With reference to the instructions of Num. 15.38–39 and Deut. 22.12 (note also Zech. 8.23).

[11] Mark 1.40–44 pars.; Mark 7.15–23/Matt. 15.11–20; Matt. 23.25–26/Luke 11.39–41.

(b) Jesus' God-talk

What was Jesus' own theo-logy, his own teaching about God and the worship of God?

Most immediately striking is the fact that Jesus evidently drew upon the *Shema* in his own teaching. According to Mark 12.28–31,[12] when asked what is the first commandment, Jesus responded by citing the *Shema* in total:

> Hear, O Israel: the Lord our God, the Lord is one; and you shall love the Lord your God with all your heart, and with all your soul, and with all your mind, and with all your strength.
>
> (NRSV)

According to the same passage, the second commandment is drawn from Leviticus 19.18: 'you shall love your neighbour as yourself' (Mark 12.31 pars.). The point to be noted here is that Jesus is remembered in earliest Christian tradition not simply for putting the love command ('love your neighbour as yourself') at the heart of his teaching (Mark 12.31 pars.); he is remembered as also putting the love command second to the primary command, to love *God* with all one's being (Mark 12.30 pars.). For Jesus the *Shema* was evidently fundamentally determinative of the whole orientation of life. It is not the case that Jesus' ethic can be boiled down to love of neighbour. On the contrary, the implication is that the two commands go together, and perhaps also that the second is only possible in long-term reality as the corollary to the first.

We may add the information already mentioned in the Introduction, that when tempted by Satan to worship him, Jesus replied explicitly, 'Worship the Lord your God, and serve only him' (Matt. 4.10/Luke 4.8). And when he was addressed as 'Good teacher', he is recalled as replying, 'Why do you call me good? No one is good but God alone' (Mark 10.17–18).

---

[12] Matthew and Mark sum up the significance of the teaching in regard to the law in different but complementary words (Matt. 22.40; Mark 12.31b). And Luke has given the teaching an intriguing twist by having the key command uttered by a lawyer, with Jesus approving (Luke 10.27–28).

The implication is clear, that for Jesus God alone is worthy of worship and of such devotion, because God alone is the source and definition of all goodness.

Also worthy of notice are the first two petitions with which Jesus began the prayer that he taught to his disciples. The first was, 'Hallowed be your name' (Matt. 6.9/Luke 11.2). Basic to the idea of 'holiness', of the adjective 'holy' and the verb 'hallow/ sanctify', is the thought of otherness, set-apartness from everyday usage. As referred to God, holiness denotes the wholly otherness of God, and provides a further rationale for the rejection of all attempts to configure God as a projection of human ideals (a man-made idol). God's know-ability to humankind, that is God in/as his name, depends on human-kind according him/his name absolute respect; anything less will simply mean that his name is not apprehended, and God is not known. This also is entirely of a piece with the affirma-tion that God is one, that Yahweh is alone Lord. For were there other worthy recipients of such devotion and commitment, the God of Israel could not demand such exclusive and total respect.

Equally noteworthy is the second petition of the Lord's Prayer, 'May your kingdom come' (Matt. 6.10/Luke 11.2). For no one can have any doubt that the main theme and emphasis of Jesus' preaching was 'the kingdom (or kingship) of God'.[13] But too few note the principal corollary, that in the kingdom of God, God is *King*, God alone; God *alone* as king, the *only* God as ruler over all (including all other so-called gods), God as the only one worthy to command complete and singular loyalty and obedience. In the kingdom of God the (human) subject owes unconditional obedience to the king; a double allegiance is impossible (Matt. 6.24/Luke 16.13). The king, and the king alone, has the power to determine the eternal destiny of his subjects (Matt. 10.28/Luke 12.4–5).

It is hard to avoid any conclusion other than that the *Shema* continued to be of central importance for Jesus during his

---

[13] See *Jesus Remembered* Ch. 12.

mission and in the teaching he both gave and lived out. Which also means that the conviction that God was one continued to be axiomatic for Jesus, a core principle from which he drew his inspiration and instruction. In short, it is hardly possible to avoid giving an affirmative answer to the question that heads this section. Yes, Jesus was a monotheist.

Yet here too more is to be said.

(c) The impression Jesus made on his disciples

The data here can be summed up by reference to three strands of the Jesus tradition: those passages that indicate in some way or other that Jesus envisaged himself as God's son; those where he is remembered as teaching with a surprising degree of self-asserted authority; and those in which he may have spoken of himself in terms of the Danielic 'one like a son of man'. For if Jesus was remembered as referring or alluding to himself in status terms beyond the ordinary, then that finding could certainly have a bearing on our central question. The references here will have to be brief, but the first two in particular command a considerable degree of agreement among New Testament scholars.

First, more than a generation ago Joachim Jeremias argued that Jesus consistently and distinctively addressed God as *Abba* ('Father'). *Abba* being a familial word, equivalent to the affectionate 'Dad' or even the childish 'Daddy', it can reasonably be inferred that Jesus perceived his relationship with God as son to father in terms of the intimacy of a family relationship.[14] For my own part, the key consideration here is the repeated testimony of Paul (Rom. 8.15–17; Gal. 4.6–7) that the *abba*-prayer was a *distinctive* feature of earliest Christian worship, and distinctive not least as attesting a sonship that the Christian pray-ers *shared with Jesus* (as 'fellow heirs with Christ'). If Paul, who would have been no stranger to Jewish prayer, could regard the *abba*-prayer as such a distinctive feature of Christian prayer,

---

[14] Jeremias, *Proclamation* 63–8. The point should not be overstated; see J. Barr, 'Abba Isn't Daddy!', *JTS* 39 (1988) 28–47.

and a sign of an inheritance shared with Jesus, then we can be confident that Jeremias' conclusion was basically sound.[15]

Here we are in effect back where we found ourselves at the end of Chapter 2: the New Testament writers' conviction that the Christian's relationship with God is intimately bound up with Jesus. For the implication is clearly that the sonship of believers is *derived* from Jesus' sonship, is a sharing in *Jesus'* sonship. Jesus can even be thought of as the eldest brother in a new family of God (Rom. 8.29).[16] Yet there is also the implication that Jesus as Son not only represents other sons before God as Father, but also represents the Father to the other sons, makes known the Father to them. This latter is an emphasis of John's Gospel,[17] but it is also present in the other Gospels, nowhere more clearly than in Matthew 11.27/Luke 10.22:

> All things have been handed over to me by my Father; and no one knows the Son except the Father, and no one knows the Father except the Son and anyone to whom the Son chooses to reveal him.　　　　　　　　　　　　　　　　　　　(NRSV)

Second, it has often been noted that Jesus was remembered as speaking with an authority that not only rivalled but even outstripped the authority usually accorded to Moses and the great prophets. One example is the 'but I say' formula that Matthew has retained in the antitheses of Matthew 5 ('You have heard it said . . ., but I say . . .'), which include radical interpretations of commandments of Moses. The phrase stands in some contrast also to the familiar formula of the prophet, 'Thus says the Lord . . .' A second example is Jesus' habit of introducing points of teaching by prefacing them with 'Amen'.[18] The word was familiar from regular liturgical usage, where the congregation

---

[15] See further *Jesus Remembered* 711–18.
[16] See further Ch. 4.6, below.
[17] See further Ch. 4.3(a), below.
[18] E.g. Mark 3.28; 8.12; 9.1 pars.; 9.41 par.; 10.15 pars.; 10.29 pars.; 11.23; 12.43 par.; 13.30 pars.; 14.9 par.; 14.18 par.; 14.25; 14.30 pars.

said 'Amen' to affirm or endorse the words of someone else.[19] But in the Gospels the term is used without exception to introduce and endorse Jesus' *own* words, presumably as a strong solemn affirmation of the importance of what was about to be said. No wonder, then, that the authority that Jesus seems thus to have claimed for his teaching made a considerable impact on his hearers – as in Mark 1.27, 'What is this? A new teaching with authority!' On the basis of such data it is highly plausible to say that in effect Jesus claimed to speak with divine authority, even as a 'spokesman for God'.[20]

The third strand of evidence is more controversial. It focuses attention on the passages where Jesus is recalled as referring to the vision of the man-like figure in the visions of Daniel 7 ('one like a son of man') in what is best understood as self-reference. The most important passage is Mark 14.61–64 (and parallels),[21] where in his trial before the Jewish council Jesus responds to the high priest's questions about his status by alluding to Daniel 7.14: 'you will see the Son of Man seated at the right hand of the Power, and coming with the clouds of heaven'. The fact that the high priest is represented as accusing Jesus of blasphemy (Mark 14.63–64 par.) reminds us immediately of the Jewish reflection about divine or heavenly intermediary figures that came close to the blasphemy of recognizing a divine presence in heaven other than God.[22] The implication is that Jesus was portraying himself in or as fulfilling the role of the man-like figure of Daniel's vision (Dan. 7.13) in taking the second throne beside the Ancient of Days in heaven (7.9, 14). In other words, a charge of blasphemy was plausible in that Jesus seemed to be placing himself among the heavenly mediators of mystic vision, and was therefore claiming a status and authority that in at

---

[19] Num. 5.22; Deut. 27.15–26; 1 Kings 1.36; 1 Chron. 16.36; Neh. 5.13; 8.6; Pss. 41.13; 72.19; 89.52; 106.48; Jer. 11.5; 28.6.

[20] Mark 9.37/Luke 9.48; Matt. 10.40; Luke 10.16. E. P. Sanders, *Jesus and Judaism* (London: SCM Press, 1985) did not hesitate to conclude that 'Jesus claimed to be spokesman for God' (271, 281).

[21] But see also Mark 8.38 pars.; 13.24–27 pars.

[22] See Ch. 3.4; and further *Jesus Remembered* 749–52, with other bibliography.

least some degree challenged the status and authority that belonged to God alone.

So we can answer the question, 'Was Jesus a monotheist?', at least initially with a straight 'Yes. Jesus was a monotheist; he confessed God as one; he proclaimed the one God's royal rule; he prayed to and encouraged his disciples to pray to this God. He worshipped God alone.' The circumstantial evidence regarding Jesus' upbringing reviewed above (a) strongly disposes the questioner towards that answer. And the clearest evidence, in Jesus' own God-talk (b), can hardly be interpreted in any other way.

Yet at the same time we can hardly ignore the evidence briefly reviewed in the final section (c). For Jesus left a huge impression of an intimacy with God as his Father that the disciples could only begin to experience as they stood with him and came to God as Father in dependence on him, as though youngsters who found it possible to stand before their father only when accompanied by their older brother. Jesus' first disciples recalled his mission and teaching as revealing God and God's will to them as never before; he spoke with the voice of God, but more clearly and definitively than either Moses or the prophets. And Jesus himself probably also drew on Daniel's vision of heavenly reality to explain his own mission and destiny. In short, even in the way the first Christians remembered Jesus they found every encouragement not only to come to God through him, but also to recognize that God had come to them through him and his mission too.

4.2 'Jesus is Lord'

Whatever we can or should say about Jesus and his mission, there can be little or no question that what the first Christians believed had happened to Jesus after his death transformed their appreciation of him completely. For they were convinced that God had raised him from the dead. This is the core affirmation of Christian faith, and it can be traced back firmly to the earliest days of the movement that stemmed from Jesus, and in particular to the visionary experiences that the first

Christians had of Jesus as risen from the dead and exalted to heaven.[23] Such belief was already a confession by the time Paul was himself converted, which was probably less than two years after Jesus' crucifixion (1 Cor. 15.3–7). And Paul was probably converted to beliefs that he had persecuted, beliefs already well established among the first members of the sect of the Nazarenes. Theirs was an astonishing belief in itself. Many Jews believed that there would be a resurrection at the end of time and before the day of last judgment; that is, a general resurrection of the dead. But the thought of one person being resurrected (not simply revived to his previous life) was unheard of. Something of mind-blowing significance had happened, and Jesus was at the centre of it.

More to the immediate point, these earliest believers were also convinced that Jesus had been taken or exalted to heaven. What had happened to Jesus was not simply a translation like that of Enoch or Elijah, nor simply a vindication such as Wisdom 5 assures the righteous they could anticipate. What then? We can safely assume that the first disciples would have searched the Scriptures to help explain and make sense of what had happened to Jesus. A key verse that shed much light for them and that evidently informed and shaped the earliest Christian reflection on the subject was Psalm 110.1:

> The Lord said to my Lord, 'Sit at my right hand, until I make your enemies a footstool for your feet'.

---

[23] Hurtado rightly emphasizes the importance of such earliest Christian experience in causing the mutation in the Jewish monotheistic tradition into Christian binitarian devotion: 'rather than trying to account for such a development as the veneration of Jesus by resort to vague suggestions of ideational borrowing from the cafeteria of heroes and demigods of the Greco–Roman world, scholars should pay more attention to this sort of religious experience of the first Christians' (*One God, One Lord* 117–22; here 121; also 126–8; also *Lord Jesus Christ* 64–74, 78; *How on Earth* Ch. 8). A. Y. Collins, 'The Worship of Jesus and the Imperial Cult', in Newman, et al. (eds), *Jewish Roots* 234–57 (here 251, 257), does not disagree but argues that the imperial cult was another catalyst in the origin of the worship of Jesus, even though, presumably, that influence did not begin to be a factor till the Gentile mission was under way.

This verse runs like a gold thread through much of the New Testament,[24] and is so interwoven into the language of the New Testament writers that it evidently was a primary starting point or stimulus for the strong strand of New Testament christ-ology summed up in the confession, 'Jesus is Lord'. The title ('lord') in itself did not necessarily signify any more than the status of a (human) master to his servant or slave; but in the context of the times, use of the title for Jesus in a cultic setting affirmed that he was being ranked alongside the gods of other cults (Asclepius, Isis, etc.), or alongside the Emperor in some degree of competition with the divine claims made for Caesar. And in the context given to the title 'Lord' (*kyrios*) by Psalm 110.1, its reference to Christ immediately indicates that in earliest Christian faith Jesus was now to be reckoned in terms similar to those used for the heavenly beings of earlier Jewish reflection, or, more precisely, to be reckoned as sharing the one God's rule. With this title Jesus is seen to be more on the side of God reach-ing out to humankind, than of humankind coming to God.

The significance of the title can be demonstrated by reference to several key texts in the first generation letters of Paul.

(a) The Yahweh texts referred to Jesus

In the many uses of *kyrios* in Paul's letters, the great majority refer to Jesus. *Kyrios* was Paul's favourite title for the exalted Jesus.[25] For example, he summarizes his gospel as the preaching

---

[24] Mark 12.36 pars.; 14.63 pars.; Acts 2.34–35; Rom. 8.34; 1 Cor. 15.25; Eph. 1.20; Col. 3.1; Heb. 1.3, 13; 8.1; 10.12; 12.2; 1 Pet. 3.22. See further particularly M. Hengel, '"Sit at My Right Hand!"': The Enthronement of Christ at the Right Hand of God', *Studies in Early Christology* (Edinburgh: T&T Clark, 1995) 119–225. Hurtado pays relatively little attention to Ps. 110.1, only briefly in *Lord Jesus Christ* 105, 179–80, 183–4. Bauckham gives it due attention and notes its 'novel exegesis and novel claim', though he regards 'at the right hand' of God's throne as sharing God's throne (*Jesus and the God of Israel* 173–9, 198 and index). Oddly enough, however, on Bauckham's argument (*Jesus and the God of Israel* 224), earliest Christian use of Ps. 110.1 does not constitute 'a christology of divine identity', since it assumes some distinction between ΥΗΨΗ (*ho kyrios*) and the Lord Christ.

[25] In the undisputed Pauline letters (excluding Ephesians and the Pastorals) 'Lord' is used in reference to Christ about 200 times.

of 'Jesus Christ as Lord' (2 Cor. 4.5), and a positive response to such preaching as 'you received the tradition of Christ Jesus as Lord' (Col. 2.6). 'Jesus is Lord' in Romans 10.9 looks like one of the earliest baptismal confessions, perhaps the earliest: 'if you confess with your lips that "Jesus is Lord" and believe in your heart that God raised him from the dead you will be saved'. The only real exceptions to the exclusive reference of *kyrios* to Jesus are a number of Old Testament passages that Paul quotes, with their original reference to the Lord (Yahweh) unaltered.[26] However, the picture becomes more complex when we realize that the Old Testament eschatological expectation of 'the day of the Lord' seems to have become the Christian hope for 'the day of our Lord Jesus Christ' (1 Cor. 1.8; 2 Cor. 1.14).[27] Still more striking is the fact that *in several instances Paul quotes an Old Testament reference to the Lord (Yahweh) and refers it to the Lord Jesus Christ.*[28]

One striking example is the passage just cited – Romans 10.9–13. The passage concludes by quoting Joel 2.32:[29] 'for everyone who calls upon the name of the Lord shall be saved' (Rom. 10.13). Now in Joel 2.32 'the Lord' is obviously Yahweh. But equally obviously in Romans 10.9–13 'the Lord' is the Lord confessed with the lips – 'Jesus is Lord.' The salvation of which Joel spoke is promised to those who confess Jesus as Lord. He is the Lord upon whose name those who believe in Jesus call. As already pointed out in Chapter 1, the fact that Paul thought of his readership in these terms is confirmed by his description of believers in the opening of his first letter to the Corinthians, as 'all those who in every place call on the name of the Lord Jesus Christ' (1 Cor. 1.2). The calling of which Joel spoke is a

---

[26] Nineteen times in the Pauline corpus.

[27] See further *Theology of Paul* 254–5.

[28] See particularly D. B. Capes, *Old Testament Yahweh Texts in Paul's Christology* (WUNT 2.47; Tübingen: Mohr Siebeck, 1992); also 'YHWH Texts and Monotheism in Paul's Christology', in Stuckenbruck and North (eds), *Early Jewish and Christian Monotheism* 120–37; Hurtado, *Lord Jesus Christ* 108–18; Bauckham, *Jesus and the God of Israel* 186–94.

[29] In the Greek version (LXX) the verse is numbered Joel 3.5.

calling on God to exercise his saving power on behalf of the remnant of Israel. So the fact that Paul refers the same verse to the exalted Jesus presumably means for Paul either that Jesus *is* Yahweh,[30] or, more likely, that Yahweh has bestowed his own unique saving power on the Lord who sits on his right side,[31] or that the exalted Jesus is himself the embodiment as well as the executive of that saving power.

The most striking example is found in the hymn or hymn-like passage in Philippians 2.5–11, already quoted in Chapter 2 in full. I repeat the climax of the hymn:

> Wherefore God exalted him to the heights
>> and bestowed on him the name that is over every name,
> that at the name of Jesus every knee should bow . . .
>> and every tongue confess that Jesus Christ is Lord,
> to the glory of God the Father.

The most remarkable feature here is the confidence that 'at the name of Jesus every knee should bow . . . and every tongue confess that Jesus Christ is Lord'. Those familiar with the scriptures of Israel would have quickly recognized the obviously deliberate echo of and allusion to Isaiah 45.23 (NRSV):

> By myself I have sworn,
>> from my mouth has gone forth in righteousness
> a word that shall not return:
> 'To me every knee shall bow,
>> every tongue shall swear.'

---

[30] As Bauckham does not hesitate to affirm (*Jesus and the God of Israel* 193, 196). But if Ps. 110.1 allows the concept of two Lords, the second given his plenipotentiary status by the first, then there is presumably no reason why a passage like Joel 2.32 should not be referred to the second Lord (see the next note).

[31] That God was understood to pass divine authority to others is indicated by the various individuals who were thought to play the role of heavenly judges – Adam and Abel (*T. Abr.* 11, 13), Melchizedek (11QMelch 13–14), Enoch and Elijah (*1 Enoch* 90.31; *Apoc. Elij.* 24.11–15) – including the saints themselves (Matt. 19.28/Luke 22.30; 1 Cor. 6.2–3). Cf. Hurtado's careful formulation: 'Early Christians saw Jesus as the *uniquely* significant agent of the one God, and in their piety they extended the exclusivity of the one God to take in God's uniquely important representative, while stoutly refusing to extend this exclusivity to any other figures' (*Lord Jesus Christ* 204).

They would also no doubt be aware that this verse was the conclusion to one of the most emphatically monotheistic passages in Israel's scriptures:

> There is no other god besides me,
> a righteous God and a Saviour;
> there is no one besides me.
>
> Turn to me and be saved,
> all the ends of the earth!
> For I am God, and there is no other.
> By myself I have sworn ...
>
> (45.21–23, NRSV)

That just this passage should be taken up in the Philippian hymn is astonishing. Was the obeisance called for by Yahweh to be given to Christ? Was the oath of fealty to the one and only God now to be given to Christ? The answer is not so straightforward as at first it may seem. For the hymn does not actually say that Jesus as Lord is to be worshipped as the one God is to be worshipped. The hymn could simply be saying that the worship of the one God is now to be expressed by confessing Jesus as Lord. Here, the final line of the hymn should not be forgotten. The obeisance and acclamation will be 'to the glory of God the Father' (Phil. 2.11).[32] As Larry Kreitzer notes, 'The very presence of such a qualifying phrase as *eis doxan theou patros* indicates something of the way in which Jewish monotheism expressed itself in the light of the exaltation of Christ.'[33] At the very least, then, the hymn asserts that the confession of Jesus as Lord is the way in which obeisance to the one God will be expressed. Jesus' Lordship is such a definitive manifestation of the saving power of God that the confession of Jesus as Lord is a confession of the one God. It is the way in which one confesses that God is one, that the oneness of God is also evident in Jesus as Lord. Should we press a little further

---

[32] In Rom. 14.11 Paul quotes Isa. 45.23 as referring to the obeisance and praise due to God.

[33] L. J. Kreitzer, *Jesus and God in Paul's Eschatology* (JSNTS 19; Sheffield: JSOT, 1987) 161.

and conclude that the hymn asserts that Jesus as Lord will be a fellow-recipient of the worship of the one God – that the one seated at God's right hand, God's plenipotentiary, is equally due the worship that should be offered only to God?[34] Who can now say precisely what the first Christians who sang or chanted such a hymn understood by it? At the very least, however, this hymn clearly affirmed that the Lord Jesus was on the other side, the divine side, of the act of worshipping the one God.

(b) 1 Corinthians 8.6

An even more striking passage comes in 1 Corinthians. In Chapter 8 Paul addresses the challenge of some Corinthian believers willing to eat food sacrificed to idols, on the grounds that 'no idol in the world really exists' and 'there is no God but one' (1 Cor. 8.4). Paul's response is riveting for several reasons:

> Even if there are so-called gods, whether in heaven or on earth, as indeed there are gods many and lords many, yet for us there is one God, the Father, from whom all things and us for him, and one Lord Jesus Christ, through whom all things and us through him.
>
> (8.5–6)

---

[34] See e.g. Hurtado, *How on Earth* 92–5, 105–7; Fee, *Pauline Christology* 396–400. Bauckham presses the point: the Philippians passage claims 'that it is in the exaltation of Jesus, his identification as YHWH in YHWH's universal sovereignty, that the unique deity of the God of Israel comes to be acknowledged as such by all creation' (*God Crucified* 53 = *Jesus and the God of Israel* 38; also 197–210). But would the acclamation given to the one whom the Lord God had made Lord at his right hand (Ps. 110.1) be any different? Bauckham insists that 'the name that is above every name' (2.9) given to the exalted Jesus is YHWH, not 'Lord', 'which is not the divine name ... but a conventional Greek *substitute* for the name' (199–202). But he forgets that the Greek *onoma* ('name') can have the force of 'title' (Matt. 10.41–42; 1 Pet. 4.16; BDAG 714), and he surprisingly plays down the force of *kyrios* as used for Christ, of which he had made so much a few pages earlier (186–94). McGrath agrees that the name given to Jesus is the name of God, but reads the text as affirming that 'God here shares his own exalted status with Jesus in a way that does not jeopardize God's ultimate supremacy ... In ancient Judaism, God could empower his agent to wield his full power and authority, *precisely because* any figure so empowered always remained by definition subject and subordinate to the one empowering him, namely God' (*The Only True God* 49–52).

For one thing, as already noted, Paul shows himself (or allows himself to be heard) to be somewhat ambivalent on the question whether the confession of God as one necessarily implies the denial of the existence of any other gods. He speaks of 'so-called gods', implying that other beings worshipped as god were not really gods, not gods in fact. But he also seems to affirm that there are 'gods many and lords many'. Perhaps he was simply acknowledging that many gods were in fact worshipped and saying in effect, Whether there are other gods or not, for us what matters is the one God revealed to Israel.

The really crucial feature, however, is that Paul seems to have taken up the *Shema*, already in effect quoted in 8.4, and to have adapted, expanded or transformed it. Where the *Shema* confessed, 'The Lord our God is one Lord', or 'the Lord our God, the Lord is one' (Deut. 6.4), Paul seems to have dismembered the confession of oneness into two parts: 'For us there is one God, the Father . . . and one Lord Jesus . . .' In view of this, how should we express the implications? That according to Paul Jesus now shares the Lordship of the one God? That Jesus as Lord expresses the Lordship of the one God? That Jesus has somehow been incorporated into the *Shema*, into the oneness of God?[35]

There is controversy at this point. Bauckham insists:[36]

the only possible way to understand Paul as maintaining monotheism is to understand him to be including Jesus in the unique identity of the one God affirmed in the *Shema*' . . . He is identifying Jesus as the 'Lord' whom the *Shema*' affirms to be one . . . the unique identity of the one God *consists of* the one God, the Father, *and* the one Lord, his Messiah.

---

[35] N. T. Wright, *The Climax of the Covenant* (Edinburgh: T&T Clark, 1991), e.g., speaks of 'christological monotheism' (114–18). Bauckham entitles the second chapter of *God Crucified* 'Christological Monotheism in the New Testament' and elaborates what he means by the term in *Jesus and the God of Israel* 184–5; see also 210–18. Fee follows Bauckham (*Pauline Christology* 89–94). Other bibliography in McGrath, *The Only True God* 114 n. 4. Richardson is more hesitant (*Paul's Language about God* 300).

[36] Bauckham, *God Crucified* 38 = *Jesus and the God of Israel* 28. For others who see here a Christian version of the *Shema* see *Jesus and the God of Israel* 211 n. 69 – including Dunn, *Christology* 180!

However, the point is not quite as clear cut as Bauckham suggests. For the question arises as to whether Paul did indeed intend to 'split the *Shema*'. It is quite possible to argue, alternatively, that Paul took up the *Shema*, already quoted in 8.4 ('there is no God but one'), only in the first clause of 8.6 (reworded as 'for us there is one God, the Father'); and to that added the *further* confession, 'and one Lord Jesus Christ'.[37] Bauckham argues that 'the addition of a unique Lord to the unique God of the *Shema*' would flatly *contradict* the uniqueness of the latter'.[38] But if anything the fuller confession of 8.6 could be said to be a more natural outworking of the primary conviction that 'the Lord (God) had said to the Lord (Christ), "Sit at my right hand . . ."' (Ps. 110.1), a confession set precisely in contrast to the gods many and lords many of Graeco–Roman worship.

Perhaps we can draw something from the prepositions used in the qualifying phrases: 'one God, *from* whom all things and us *for* him'; 'one Lord, *through* whom all things and us *through* him'. A distinction remains between the one God and the one Lord. The one *God* is not only referred to as 'the Father' but is also seen as the *source* and origin of everything, and as the *goal* towards whom believers should direct themselves;[39] whereas the one *Lord* is referred to in terms of agency, the *mediating agency* through whom all things and believers have effective being. We seem to be back in the sort of distinction that the Wisdom tradition and Philo strove to maintain, between God as the ultimate and unknowable source of being, and God making himself known through his acts of creation and what he created. This sharing of divine identity (to use Bauckham's

---

[37] So McGrath, *The Only True God* 38–44: 'When the oneness of God is coupled with another assertion of oneness in this way, we must look carefully to determine whether we are indeed dealing with a splitting of the Shema that is without parallel, or an addition of a second clause *alongside* the Shema, which is not in fact unparalleled in Jewish literature' (40).

[38] Bauckham, *God Crucified*; and more emphatically in *Jesus and the God of Israel* 212–13.

[39] Elsewhere Paul takes for granted that Israel's confession of God as one is still his own confession – Rom. 3.30; 1 Cor. 8.4; Gal. 3.20; Eph. 4.6.

terminology) is equivalent to the way Wisdom and Word were conceived of as sharing divine identity – precisely by making a distinction between origin and agency.[40]

However 1 Corinthians 8.6 should be interpreted, it remains a riveting and mind-blowing fact that the Jesus who had lived only about 30 years before this letter was written was being seen as synonymous with that divine agency. Where Paul could think of worship and prayer offered to God in Jesus and through Jesus, he also evidently thought of God acting through Jesus and making himself known in and through Jesus. The passage 'through' Jesus was a two-way passage, from humankind to God, but also from God to humankind.

(c) 1 Corinthians 15.24–28

For any inquiry into whether the first Christians worshipped Jesus, the fact that Paul spoke of Jesus sharing or expressing the one God's Lordship is bound to be a powerful factor in determining the inquiry's outcome. Yet Paul also expresses himself in other terms on the same point. In various passages he uses the formula, 'The God and Father of our Lord Jesus Christ'.[41] The striking feature is that Paul speaks of God not simply as the God of Christ, but as 'the *God* . . . of our *Lord* Jesus Christ'. Even as Lord, Jesus acknowledges God not only as his Father but also as his God. Here it becomes plain that the *kyrios* title is not so much a way of *identifying* Jesus with God, as a way of *distinguishing* Jesus from God. It cannot be unimportant that Paul can use both *kyrios* Yahweh texts in reference to Christ (a), and at the same time can speak of God as 'the God of our Lord'.[42]

---

[40] Both C. K. Barrett, *The First Epistle to the Corinthians* (London: A. & C. Black, 1968) 193, and W. Schrage, *Der erste Brief an die Korinther* (EKK VII/2; Zurich: Benziger, 1995) 243, note that the language indicates a close relation between Christ and God, but not an identity of the two.

[41] See Introduction n. 2.

[42] Note also 1 Cor. 3.23 – 'You are Christ's, and Christ is God's'; and 11.3 – 'the head of Christ is God'. Bauckham seems to ignore this material, and Hurtado refers to it only as evidence of the 're-identification of God by reference to Jesus' (*Origins* 74; also 108).

Most notable in this connection is 1 Corinthians 15.24–28. In effect it is the nearest we have in the New Testament to an exposition of the crucial text, Psalm 110.1, that so influenced the first Christians:

> Then comes the end, when he [Christ] hands over the kingdom to God the Father, after he has destroyed every ruler and every authority and power. For he must reign until 'he has put all his enemies under his feet' [Ps. 8.6]. The last enemy to be destroyed is death. For 'he [God] has put all things in subjection under his feet' [Ps. 8.6]. But when it says 'All things are put in subjection', it is plain that this does not include the one who put all things in subjection under him. When all things are subjected to him, then the Son himself will also be subjected to the one who put all things in subjection under him, so that God may be all in all. (NRSV, adapted)

What is particularly striking here is the way the Christ's heavenly rule at God's right hand is portrayed. The kingship of the Lord Christ is undoubtedly thought of as complete and final. All things, all cosmic powers, every enemy, even the power of the last enemy (death) will be subjected to Christ. He will reign until the end.[43] But Paul also makes it clear that there is a more ultimate kingship, that of God the Father. At the end the Lord Christ will hand over the kingdom to God, and himself be subjected (*hypotagēsetai*) to God who subjected (*hypotagē*) all (other) things to him, 'so that God may be all in all' (15.28). This again has echoes of Philo's understanding of the Logos: that the Logos is the ultimate, as far as humankind can reach out to God, and as far as God can come to humankind, but that God is always beyond the Logos. So with the Lordship of Christ. In an important sense no acknowledgment of dignity and status is too high to indicate his significance. But even when the highest honour can be accorded to him or recognized

---

[43] This is what Bauckham refers to when he argues that 'Jesus' sovereignty over "all things"' indicates that for Paul Jesus shares in the identity of God as the unique universal ruler (*Jesus and the God of Israel* 21–3).

as already his, even then the qualification has to be added: but God (the Father) is still beyond; God will only be 'all in all' when the Lord Christ is seen to be included in the 'all in all'.[44]

What does this say about worshipping the Lord Jesus Christ? That he should receive honour and glory due to God alongside God, though as an expression of the ultimate honour and glory due only to God (Phil. 2.11). That the one Lord Jesus Christ is integral to the creedal confession of the one God, that he embodies the divine agency by which God accomplishes his creative and redemptive purposes, though praise to the source and origin of all things should be given only to the one God and Father (1 Cor. 8.6). That the worship due to God the 'all in all' should always be beyond the submission and devotion given to the Lord Christ (1 Cor. 15.28). Whether the first Christians would have expressed themselves in just these terms is hardly certain, but the care with which Paul in particular stated his *kyrios* christology should certainly give us pause before we answer a straightforward 'Yes' or 'No' to our central question.

---

[44] Unfortunately Bauckham does not seem to think it necessary to consider the whole passage (1 Cor. 15.24–28), including 15.28. Hurtado likewise passes over the passage too lightly (*Lord Jesus Christ* 104–5, 600). Contrast earlier attempts to clarify the relation between Jesus and God, where discussion of 1 Cor. 15.24–28 plays a central role; particularly W. Thüsing, *Per Christum in Deum* (Münster: Aschendorff, 1965) Ch. 6; Kreitzer, *Jesus and God* Ch. 3, particularly 158–60. See also A. C. Thiselton, *The First Epistle to the Corinthians* (NIGTC; Grand Rapids: Eerdmans, 2000) 1236–9, and Schrage, *Korinther* VII/4 (Benziger, 2001) 213–17, who both note how important the passage was in the early Trinitarian controversy over the subordination of the Son. O. Cullmann, *The Christology of the New Testament* (London: SCM Press, 1959) regarded 1 Cor. 15.28 as 'the key to all New Testament Christology', understanding it in functional rather than ontological terms: 'It is only meaningful to speak of the Son in view of God's revelatory action, not in view of his being' (emphasized by Cullmann). Somewhat surprisingly Fee attempts a resolution by arguing that 15.28 does not refer to Christ's *person* but rather his *role* or function, whereas 8.6 has in view Jesus' 'divine identity' (*Pauline Christology* 113–14).

(d) Did Paul persecute the first Christians because of their Jesus devotion?

As part of his argument that the first Christians worshipped Jesus from the earliest days of the movement that became 'Christianity', Hurtado finds strong support in the likelihood 'that prominent among his [Saul's/Paul's] reasons for proceeding against the early Jewish Christians was his outrage over their claims about Jesus and their reverence of him'. Prior to Paul's conversion, Hurtado maintains, it can be inferred 'that his [Paul's] previous opposition had been directed against just the sort of view of Jesus that he felt divinely directed to embrace in his conversion'.[45]

Hurtado's argument, however, is surprisingly weak. Of course it can be inferred that what Paul experienced as his encounter with the risen and exalted Jesus on the Damascus road radically changed his mind about Jesus. Paul's own admission that Jews found the proclamation of Christ crucified to be a stumbling block (1 Cor. 1.23) strongly suggests that prior to his conversion such had been his attitude too. And many justifiably deduce from Galatians 3.13 that most Jews would regard the crucified Jesus as accursed by God. Obviously Paul's views on the subject changed dramatically, as he himself implies in Philippians 3.7–11. But the argument that Paul's pre-Christian dismissal of earliest Christian claims for Jesus can and should be read as outrage over early Christian *cultic devotion* of Jesus goes well beyond the evidence and is in grave danger of the classic fault of *petitio principii*; that is, of begging the question and reading into the data what one wants to read out from it. But since Hurtado builds so much on this argument a short excursus is called for to consider it.

For one thing, in asking why Saul/Paul persecuted the first Christians, Hurtado ignores almost completely the chief reason Paul himself gives for his persecuting. In Philippians 3.6 Paul

---

[45] *How on Earth* 34–6; also 69–74, *Lord Jesus Christ* 175–6, and the more detailed argument of 'Early Jewish Opposition to Jesus-Devotion', *JTS* 50 (1999) 35–58, reproduced in *How on Earth* Ch. 7 (here 168–77).

explicitly states that his persecuting was motivated by and expressive of his 'zeal' – 'as to zeal, a persecutor of the church'. The implication of Paul's only other explicit recollection of his pre-Christian past and conversion is to the same effect:

> You have heard of my way of life previously in Judaism, that in excessive measure I persecuted the church of God and tried to destroy it; and that I progressed in Judaism beyond many of my contemporaries among my people, being exceedingly zealous for my ancestral traditions. (Gal. 1.13–14)

The implication is clear: that Paul's persecution of the first Christians had been of a piece with his Pharisaic zeal for the law and the traditions of the fathers, the Halakhah, the 'zeal' being the same 'zeal' that he referred to in Philippians 3.6. This can only mean that Paul had persecuted the first Christians because he saw them as some sort of threat to his (fundamentalist) understanding of what being 'in Judaism' demanded of Jews, their loyalty to the law and adherence to the Pharisaic halakhoth. That we find it hard to fill out Paul's recollection here from what we know of the first Christians should not justify bypassing Paul's most explicit statement on the subject. I attempt to do some filling out in terms of the Hellenist Christians' openness to Gentiles (most explicit in Acts 11.20–21) being seen as a threat to Israel's set-apartness to God and from other nations; and I have shown that this is the direction in which the tradition of 'zeal' in Israel and early Judaism firmly points.[46] But a Pharisee as zealous as Paul might well have taken violence-justifying offence at what he perceived, rightly or wrongly, to be unacceptable disregard for the law by other Jews. The tradition of Jewish zeal certainly includes various examples of such offence and such reaction.

---

[46] See my *Beginning from Jerusalem* #25.2; Hurtado does not refer to my earlier treatment, particularly 'Paul's Conversion – A Light to Twentieth Century Disputes', in J. Ådna, et al. (eds), *Evangelium – Schriftauslegung – Kirche*; P. Stuhlmacher FS (Göttingen: Vandenhoeck & Ruprecht, 1997) 77–93.

Second, it should be remembered that Jewish believers remained largely undisturbed in Jerusalem for most of the period 30–62 CE. The spasms of persecution are not recalled as particularly motivated by hostility to Christ-devotion,[47] though the final vision of Stephen could have been a factor in his case (Acts 7.55–56). Even so, the fact that the bulk of Jewish believers in Jerusalem could subsequently be described as 'all zealous for the law' (21.20) suggests that their reverence of Jesus did not incite open opposition from the Jewish authorities in Jerusalem. Despite Hurtado, it remains significant that explicit Jewish objection to claims of deity for Jesus do appear in the New Testament, but for the first time and only in John's Gospel (John 5.18; 10.33), one of the latest of the New Testament writings, and almost certainly reflecting a post-70 situation.

Third, we know from 1 Corinthians 1.23, and by inference from Galatians 3.13, what it was about the earliest christology that offended the Jews.[48] It was the claim that Jesus, a crucified felon, was Messiah and the instrument of God's blessing. Hurtado notes the 'conspicuous silence' of Paul in that he 'shows no need to reiterate and defend either beliefs in Jesus' exalted status or the characteristic cultic reverence given to him'; 'there were no challenges to the exalted status of Jesus asserted by Paul's gospel or to the devotional practices by which Jesus was reverenced in Paul's churches'.[49] The point for him is, justifiably, that Paul's christology should not be seen as a development or departure from the earlier Jewish Christian beliefs and practice. But he resists the equally justifiable inference that such beliefs and practices were not seen as particularly controversial or objectionable to

---

[47] Acts 6.11–14 and 8.1–3; 12.1–3; 1 Thess. 2.14–16.

[48] Capes observes that 'no sure evidence exists regarding what non-believing Jews may have thought about Paul's Christology beyond (1 Cor. 1.23)' ('YHWH Texts and Monotheism' 134). This may be counted as an 'own goal', since it both (1) undermines Hurtado's argument, and (2) ignores the obvious point that we *do* have evidence of Jewish opposition to earliest Christian views of Christ, but *not* of any Jewish hostility to early Christian claims for Jesus as violating the uniqueness of God.

[49] *Lord Jesus Christ* 165–7; also 135–6, 172–3.

most Jews of Paul's time.[50] Had they been so it would almost certainly have been referred to or reflected in the letters (Galatians, Romans) where Paul engages most directly and sharply with more traditional Jewish beliefs as they impinged on his mission. The facts that the main ground of dispute and contention was over the law and its applicability to Gentile believers, that this is so clearly evident in Paul's letters, and that the only opposition to christology referred to is to Christian proclamation of a crucified Messiah, hardly give credibility to Hurtado's thesis.

In contrast, Hurtado's attempt to find support for his thesis in 1 Corinthians 12.3 and 2 Corinthians 3—4 shows how weak is his case. The fact that Paul could envisage someone crying out, 'Let Jesus be cursed', apparently under inspiration and within a worship situation (1 Cor. 12.3), is open to various explanations, of which an official curse by Jewish authorities is not the most likely.[51] And in 2 Corinthians 3—4 Paul gives no hint as to his reasons for his own former hostility to the first Christians.

In short, the argument for a very early Christ-devotion among the first Christians is not helped or strengthened by the reasons for Paul's pre-Christian persecution of the first Christians. If anything, the 'conspicuous silence' of Paul as to the controversial character of his christology implies that it was not so very controversial for both the first Christians and for most Jews of the time.

4.3 Word, Wisdom and Spirit

In Chapter 3 we concluded that the wisdom writers and sages of Israel and early Judaism understood the Spirit, divine

---

[50] I addressed the issue earlier in 'How Controversial was Paul's Christology?', in M. C. de Boer (ed.), *From Jesus to John: Essays on Jesus and New Testament Christology*; M. de Jonge FS (JSNTS 84; Sheffield: JSOT, 1993) 148–67. McGrath also insists that 'there is no evidence that belief in a supreme mediator or agent of God was controversial within Judaism'; and observes that Frances Young also notes the lack of awareness of a 'Christological problem' on the part of the NT authors (*The Only True God* 47, 52, 116 n. 23).

[51] See e.g. the full discussion in Thiselton, *1 Corinthians* 918–24.

Wisdom, and the Logos as different and complementary ways of speaking about God in his interaction with his creation and his people. They were variously used as ways of speaking of God's immanence without infringing on his transcendent otherness. The New Testament writers were no doubt aware of this and knowingly drew on these ways of speaking of God's action and revelation as they strove to express the significance of Christ and of what God had accomplished through him. The most obvious example is the prologue to John's Gospel, where the assertion is made explicitly, 'the Word became flesh' (John 1.14); that is, became Jesus of Nazareth. In the other cases the drawing on wisdom language to refer to Christ is more controversial; but from the middle of the twentieth century there has been a widespread recognition that 'Wisdom christology' was one of the main strands of earliest Christian theological reflection.[52] And the relation of Christ to the Spirit has always been somewhat problematic to formulate adequately.

We will look briefly at all three ways of speaking about God's interaction and how they were applied to Christ or adapted to speak of him, starting with the clearest example – John 1.1–18.

(a) Logos christology

John 1.1–18 is the classic expression of Christian Logos christology:

---

[52] I may refer to my following studies, all with bibliography: *Christology* Ch. 6; *Theology of Paul* 272–5; *Beginning from Jerusalem* 805 n. 272; also B. Witherington, *Jesus the Sage: The Pilgrimage of Wisdom* (Edinburgh: T&T Clark, 1994) Ch. 6. The large-scale consensus is critiqued by Fee, *Pauline Christology* (particularly 319–25, 595–619). But (1) he almost entirely ignores the parallel passages (John 1.1–18; Heb. 1.1–3) where the echoes of wisdom language are clearer and indicate that this line of reflection was well established in earliest Christianity; (2) he makes a highly questionable differentiation between personified Wisdom and wisdom as a divine attribute; and (3) he questions whether Paul even knew the Wisdom of Solomon, despite listing (Pauline!) 'allusions' to this work (620–6) familiar to Pauline scholars for more than a century. The unwillingness to recognize echo and allusion in Pauline use of OT and early Jewish literature is a retrograde step.

In the beginning was the Word,
and the Word was with God,
and the Word was God.
He was in the beginning with God.
All things came into being through him,
and no created thing came into being without him.

. . .

And the Word became flesh and dwelt among us,
and we have seen his glory,
the glory as of the Father's only Son.

. . .

No one has ever seen God. It is the one and only, God [or Son],
who is close to the Father's heart,
who has made him known.

The dependence on Israel's Logos theology is evident, not least the deliberate echo of the account of creation in Genesis 1 – creation by the divine fiat, 'God said, "Let there be . . ."', creation by the divine word. As we saw in Chapter 3, the metaphorization of God's speech[53] into the Word was very familiar to Israel's theologians and sages. So the Johannine hymn or poem was obviously taking up and developing further this metaphor, this way of speaking about God's action in creation and revelation and salvation.

An interesting and not irrelevant question thus arises, as to whether we should translate the opening pronouns as 'he'. The question arises since prior to John the Word is personalized but not genderized ('he' is used because *logos* is a masculine noun). Moreover, as we shall see below (b), the language of the prologue is drawn equally if not more from Israel's Wisdom reflection, and Wisdom (*sophia*) is feminine. The issue is of some importance, because the translation 'he' could be taken to imply that the poem/hymn is speaking of Jesus as such from the beginning.[54] How best, then, to read the prologue?

---

[53] Contemporary linguistic philosophers would speak of God's speech-act.
[54] Some translations (or better, paraphrases) actually so translate.

From a straightforward reading of John's Gospel the answer would seem to be obvious. For in John's Gospel Jesus speaks consistently as one who was conscious of his personal pre-existence with the Father. For example, he speaks of the glory he had in God's presence before the world existed (John 17.5); Isaiah saw his glory in the Temple (12.41). Jesus asserts simply but bluntly, 'Before Abraham was, I am' (8.58), the 'I am' echoing God's own self-referential formula.[55] And he speaks regularly of his having been sent by God, his Father,[56] from heaven 'into the world' (3.17; 10.36; 17.18).[57]

Yet some hesitation remains. For John clearly felt free to attribute to Jesus words and sentiments that Jesus himself probably never uttered while on earth. As most commentators realize, had the great 'I am' sayings been uttered by Jesus during his mission in Galilee and Judea, they would hardly have been so ignored by the other Evangelists. It is much more likely that John has developed a portrayal of Jesus, on the basis of such traditional material as, in this case, Mark 6.50,[58] a portrayal that makes clear how the significance of Jesus should be seen, in John's eyes, rather than simply how Jesus was remembered.

Does such a consideration merely move the question of Jesus' personal pre-existence from being a historically questionable description of *Jesus'* own self-consciousness to *John's* perception that Jesus as such had been with God? That is certainly plausible. The alternative would be to say that John has elaborated the rich poetic metaphors used to describe the Logos, and that in transforming the Creator–Logos image into a Father–Son

---

[55] See e.g. Bauckham, *God Crucified* 55 = *Jesus and the God of Israel* 40; and further 'Monotheism and Christology in the Gospel of John', in R. N. Longenecker (ed.), *Contours of Christology in the New Testament* (Grand Rapids: Eerdmans, 2005) 148–66. McGrath argues that the 'I am' statements of the Johannine Jesus constitute a further example of 'God's agent being given the divine name in order to be empowered for his mission' (*The Only True God* 61–3).

[56] John 4.34; 5.23, 24, 30, 36, 37, 38; 6.29, 38, 39, 44, 57; 7.16, 18, 28, 29, 33; 8.16, 18, 26, 29, 42; 9.4; 11.42; 12.44, 45, 49; 13.16, 20; 14.24; 15.21; 16.5; 17.3, 8, 21, 23, 25; 20.21.

[57] See further Hurtado, *Lord Jesus Christ* 365–89.

[58] See my 'John's Gospel and the Oral Gospel Tradition' (forthcoming).

image John has given the poetic metaphor of God's immanence its richest and most elaborate expression.[59] The genius of the creator of the poem/hymn would then be that 1.14 comes as a dramatic shock in the story of the Logos. Prior to 1.14 it was the Logos through whom the world was created, which was conceived as being the true light. As we shall see in the next section, prior to 1.14 nothing is said in the poem/hymn that would be strange to a Hellenistic Jew familiar with the Jewish reflection on the immanence of God.[60] It is with 1.14 that the shockingly new is expressed: that the Logos became *flesh*, became a man, Jesus of Nazareth. Properly speaking, then, it is only with 1.14 that Jesus as such comes into the story. To be somewhat pedantic, according to the Johannine prologue, Jesus is not the Word; he is the Word become flesh. At the same time, the point should not be pushed too far. For John 1.14 also asserts that Jesus reveals what the true character of the Logos is, Jesus is the clearest expression of God's immanence, the one who makes visible the invisible God. In other words, and the point is important, *it is not so much that the personification language used of the Logos is now used of Jesus. It is rather that Jesus reveals the personal character of the Logos, a character that previously could only be expressed in personification terms.*

The success of the prologue in communicating its claim therefore depends on the background theology of Israel's reflection on the Word. In other words, John must have assumed that his readers would think of the Word as a way of speaking about God acting. The Word is the expression of God, the unspoken thought of God coming to verbal expression. Hence the opening attribution of creation to the Word; that is, to the divine fiat. Hence too the understanding of the Word as manifesting

---

[59] This move was subsequently echoed when the Nicene Creed shifted the emphasis from the early patristic focus on Logos christology to Son christology.

[60] Cf. Augustine's famous comment that from his reading of the Platonists he was familiar with all that the Johannine prologue said; what he did not find was that 'he came to what was his own, and they ... gave him no welcome'; and what he did not read in the same books was that 'the Word was made flesh and came to dwell among us' (*Confessions* VII.9).

divine glory (1.14), indeed as manifesting God, as making the unseen and un-seeable God[61] known, or literally as expounding (*exegēgēsato*) God (1.18). For in effect the claim of Jewish theology is that the Word is the self-revelation of God, the way God makes himself known. And on that claim John in turn builds in asserting that the Word became incarnate in or as Jesus, so that Jesus is the epitome and summation of that self-revelation. This is presumably why the poem/hymn does not hesitate to speak of Jesus as the only Son in intimate personal relationship with God as Father, and not only so but also as 'the one and only, God' (1.18).[62] Here, we may infer, the Johannine prologue has found itself in the same tension as Philo, when he spoke of the Logos as 'the second God' (*Quaestiones et Solutiones in Genesin* 2.62).[63] In both cases, the attempt is evidently being made to assert that the Logos is as close to God as can be imagined, that the Logos is God to the extent that God can possibly be known.

The major breakthrough that the Johannine prologue makes, then, is that it identifies the Logos with the man Jesus Christ. It brings to expression the concept of *incarnation*. The ancients had no problem with the thought of the gods appearing in the likeness of human beings. But to '*become* flesh' was a step beyond them. And the wisdom writers of Israel could think of Wisdom becoming or at least being identified with the Torah. But to identify Wisdom with a particular person was a step

---

[61] That God cannot be seen is a fundamental of Jewish thought – e.g. Exod. 33.20; Deut. 4.12; Sir. 43.31; Philo, *Post.* 168–9; Josephus, *Jewish War* 7.346.

[62] Both the text and its rendering are unclear and much disputed. *Monogenēs theos* is the more difficult reading, and (for that reason) is favoured by the majority. If so, should we translate 'a/the only begotten God', or 'a uniquely begotten deity', or 'the unique one, who is divine'? Or is the reading *monogenēs huios*, 'the one and only Son'? Or indeed, *monogenēs*, 'the utterly unique One'? See e.g. BDAG 658; J. F. McHugh, *John 1–4* (ICC; London: T&T Clark, 2009) 69–70, 110–12; McGrath, *The Only True God* 64–6.

[63] Hurtado is correct in noting that in Jewish tradition a statement like 'Wisdom was God' is never made (*Lord Jesus Christ* 367); here the closer parallel with John 1.1c ('the Word was God/god') is given by Philo.

beyond them too.[64] Yet this is what the Johannine prologue does. Jesus is the Word, God's creative speech, God's revelatory and redemptive action, become flesh. As the identification of divine Wisdom with the *Torah* was an evangelistic pitch (Here is where you will find the Wisdom you are looking for and need),[65] so John's identification of the Word with Jesus was evangelistic. John was saying that if you look at Jesus, his mission, death and resurrection, you will see the glory of God; you will hear God's word, God himself speaking to you; you will be drawn into an intimacy with God that nowhere else is possible. You will see the unseen God in and through Jesus; you will encounter God in and through Jesus.

No wonder, then, that the Jesus of John's Gospel is accused of making himself equal to God (John 5.18), indeed of making himself God (10.33). For the intimacy of the relationship between Jesus and God, the bound-togetherness of the Son and the Father, the mutual indwelling of each in the other, is all a way of saying that Jesus really is the Word of God, really is God speaking, though speaking in and through useless flesh (1.13; 3.6; 6.63). And no wonder that the Gospel climaxes in Thomas' worshipful confession, 'My Lord and my God' (20.28).

In short, John's Gospel shows very clearly why our question, 'Did the first Christians worship Jesus?', is so difficult to answer adequately. For Jesus was understood very early on as the human face of God, as the one who made the unseen God known and known more clearly and fully than he had ever been known before. In a real sense that the first Christians could only explain inadequately, to be in the presence of Jesus was to be in the

---

[64] In his allegorizing treatment of the Torah, Philo was happy to speak of such figures as Sarah as symbolizing wisdom (F. H. Colson, *Philo* [LCL, 10 vols; Cambridge, MA: Harvard University Press, 1962] 10.413–18); but this is far from 'incarnation'. The fact that ben Sira praises the high priest, Simon ben Onias (Sir. 50), in language already used of Wisdom (Sir. 24) may indicate that he saw Simon as expressing the same Wisdom, but as 'an incarnation of Wisdom' (C. H. T. Fletcher-Louis, 'The Worship of Divine Humanity as God's Image and the Worship of Jesus', in Newman, et al. (eds), *Jewish Roots* 112–28; here 115–19) presses the parallels too far.

[65] See further Ch. 3.3(b).

presence of God – not, be it noted, in the presence of *a* god, but in the presence of *God*. The aim was still as with Israel's Logos theology: to affirm a position for the Logos as close as possible to God, to the extent that they could easily be confused with each other; to assert that the Logos was truly God himself speaking and acting. That is why the Johannine Jesus can say that he is to be honoured (worshipped?) just as the Father is honoured (John 5.23). At the same time we should also note that John did not abandon all reserve on the subject. Jesus was the Son and not the Father. It was still the Father who is to be worshipped (4.23–24).[66] So even when the evidence pushes us towards a positive answer to our question, we should not forget that John's Gospel is a particular elaboration of Israel's Logos theology, and that John too endeavoured to maintain a balance between the thought of Jesus both *as* God and as *not* God the Father, the incarnate Word as the most definitive revelation of God.

(b) Wisdom christology

Anyone familiar with the way lady Wisdom is portrayed in Jewish tradition will appreciate that the prologue of John's Gospel also draws heavily on key strands of Jewish reflection on Wisdom. Like the Word in John 1.1, Wisdom was present when God made the world (Wisd. 9.9), and it was through Wisdom that the world was created (Prov. 3.19; Wisd. 8.4–6). Like the Word in John 1.4, Wisdom was conceived to be the true light.[67] Like the Word in John 1.11, Wisdom sought a dwelling place among the children of men, but found none (*1 Enoch* 42.2). Like the Word in John 1.14, Wisdom had been told to pitch her tent in Jacob (Sir. 24.8). Similarly the rather striking terms to describe the Son in Hebrews 1.3 – 'he is the radiance (*apausgama*) of God's glory and the stamp (*charaktēr*) of his nature' – are best explained as drawn from language used

---

[66] Note the extensive usage of *proskynein* in John 4.20–24 (9 times); see further Ch. 1.1.

[67] Wisd. 7.26; cf. Philo, *Opif.* 33; *Conf.* 60–3; *Som.* 1.75.

to describe Wisdom.[68] So it makes good sense to recognize the same influence in passages where Paul asserts that it was through the one Lord Jesus Christ that all things came into being (1 Cor. 8.6), that he is the image of the invisible God, the first-born of all creation, that it was in him, through him and for him that all things were created, and that he is before all things and in him all things hold together (Col. 1.15–17).[69] For this again is language that is given its currency in such contexts by reference to Wisdom, 'the image of God's goodness' (Wisd. 7.26), the firstborn of God's creative work (Prov. 8.22, 25). Divine Wisdom and/or the Word were naturally understood to have been present before creation and were characteristically understood as the agency by which God created the cosmos. Wisdom (and Word) were equally thought of as penetrating throughout the world, the divine force by which the world was sustained, the rationale by which human beings could live to best effect.[70] The thought in the theology of Israel and early Judaism was never of Wisdom (or Word) as separate beings from God, able to be conceived as independent personalities from God. Rather they were the presence of God in the world, God acting upon the world, the God-impressed moral and rational fabric without which the world and society cannot properly function as God intended.

In fact we are very close to the Logos christology of John just reviewed, even if neither Paul nor Hebrews is quite as bold and explicit as John. The points to be made are similar. Earliest Christian Wisdom christology took up the wisdom imagery and metaphor and applied it to Jesus. Not only that, it presented Jesus as the personal expression of the divine Wisdom whose personality previously could only be expressed in personification imagery. To be pedantic, again, Jesus as such was not Wisdom, but was Wisdom embodied in/incarnated as a man; or alternatively expressed, 'the fullness of deity dwelt

---

[68] The clearest examples are Wisd. 7.26 and Philo, *Plant.* 18.
[69] See again n. 52, above.
[70] See further my *Christology* 164–6, 217–18.

bodily' in him (Col. 2.9). So far as the deity of Christ is concerned, the use of such metaphorical language brings with it the same ambiguities and ambivalence as in Jewish reflection on Wisdom. And presumably with the same or similar effect. If Wisdom is a way of saying that God acted wisely in what he created, then Jesus embodies/incarnates that same Wisdom. If Wisdom is a way of speaking of the invisible God, then Jesus can be said to make visible the invisible God (Col. 1.15). To put it more provocatively, to speak of Jesus as Wisdom (or Logos) is inadequate, unless we realize that Wisdom/Logos is a way of speaking about God. What these first Christian theologians were endeavouring to say was no less than that in some real sense, Jesus is *God* acting and outgoing; Jesus brings to visible expression the very purpose and character of God himself. Jesus is not only firstborn among many sons, he is the firstborn of all being; he embodies not only the reaching up of humankind to God, but also the reaching down from God to humankind.

In regard to our central question, Paul seems further from a positive answer than John, but the ambiguity that causes the question to be posed in the first place is already evident in Paul. If the corollary of Wisdom christology is that Jesus was (to be) worshipped, then presumably the corollary is that the worship was to be offered to Jesus as divine Wisdom, Jesus as God in that God had revealed himself in and through Jesus. Or, to be more precise, it was God who was to be worshipped in that he had made himself known in and through Jesus. The worship was both informed and enabled by Jesus, by the revelation of God in and through Jesus. It is some sort of ambivalent statement such as this that the earliest Wisdom and Word christologies push us towards.

(c) Spirit christology

With Spirit christology the issues become still more complex. For the Spirit was from the beginning a way of speaking of God's life-giving action in creating humankind (Gen. 2.7), of God's presence throughout the cosmos (Ps. 139.7). So the Spirit of God was, like Wisdom and Word, a way of speaking of the divine immanence, an earlier and more pervasive way of so speaking, but not dissimilar in intent and function, as the parallels in Wisdom 9.10 and 17 illustrate. Consequently we might have expected that as Wisdom and Word were as it were absorbed into Christ – Christ as the embodiment of divine Wisdom, Christ as the incarnation of the divine Word – so it would be with Spirit. Should we not speak of a Spirit christology, as we do of a Wisdom or a Logos christology? Did the implicit binitarianism of the Jewish conception of Wisdom and Word not resolve itself into a very early Christian binitarianism, including Jesus within the concept of God in his self-revelation? And, if so, should we not deduce that Christ was seen also to fulfil the role of bringing the divine presence into human experience that had hitherto been filled by the Spirit of God?

The answer, actually, is no. For while we see in more than one New Testament writing a conception of God's action and revelation in and through the life, death and resurrection of Christ framed in terms drawn from Wisdom and Word theology, we do not find the same thing happening in Spirit terms. The Gospel writers hardly hesitate to ascribe Jesus' mission to his anointing by the Holy Spirit,[71] and Paul, despite few references to Jesus' mission on earth, probably reflects the same emphasis (2 Cor. 1.21–22). More striking is the hesitation that Paul seems to display in avoiding explicitly attributing Jesus' resurrection to the power of the Spirit. Paul had no doubt that the final resurrection would be accomplished by the power of the Spirit (Rom. 8.11), the Spirit transforming the body of this existence into the 'spiritual body' (1 Cor. 15.44–46). Yet in passages such as Romans 1.4, 6.4 and 8.11 he seems to avoid formulations that would attribute Jesus' resurrection to the same Spirit.[72] Perhaps he thought that the exaltation of Jesus to the right hand of God was an exaltation also over the Spirit

---

[71] Mark 1.10–11 pars.; John 1.32–33; Acts 10.38.

[72] See further, and for what follows, my *Christology* 141–7; but see also Fatehi, *The Spirit's Relation to the Risen Lord* 245–62.

(cf. Acts 2.33). But that would probably be too crass a way of expressing what Paul was doing.

The issue can only be clarified if we take note of three features of Paul's treatment of the Spirit:

1 Although he speaks of the Spirit regularly as 'the Spirit of God',[73] he also speaks of 'the Spirit of Christ' and 'the Spirit of God's Son'.[74] This presumably means that the Spirit of God is to be recognized as the Spirit that empowered Jesus and characterized his mission and that brings to expression in believers the same sonship and grace in those committed to God through Jesus (Rom. 8.15–17; Gal. 5.22–23).

2 He refrains from speaking of the Spirit as given by Jesus, whereas he regularly describes *God* as the one who gives the Spirit.[75] This, despite the formulation of Acts 2.33 (the exalted Christ poured out the Spirit on the day of Pentecost), and the implication that it was Jesus who baptized in Spirit in fulfilment of the Baptist's prophecy;[76] whereas when Paul talks of believers having been baptized in the Spirit he uses the divine passive (1 Cor. 12.13).

3 Paul does however speak of Christ as the last Adam having become (in his resurrection) 'life-giving spirit/Spirit'. What is so striking here is that 'life-giving' is elsewhere understood as distinctively the role of the Spirit,[77] as subsequently confessed in the creed – the Spirit, 'the Lord and giver of life'.

What follows from all this? First, that Paul was prepared to redefine the role of the Spirit in terms of the character of Jesus, or, probably better, in terms of the character of God as revealed in Jesus' mission and death. Second, that he did not understand Jesus to have taken over the role of God in giving his own Spirit to humankind. And third, that he merged the ongoing activity

---

[73] Rom. 8.9, 11, 14; 1 Cor. 2.11, 14; 3.16; 6.11; 7.40; 12.3; etc.

[74] Rom. 8.9; Gal. 4.6; Phil. 1.19.

[75] 1 Cor. 2.12; 2 Cor. 1.21–22; 5.5; Gal. 3.5; 4.6; Eph. 1.17; 1 Thess. 4.8.

[76] Mark 1.8 pars.; and again Acts 1.6 and 11.16.

[77] Note particularly John 6.63 and 2 Cor. 3.6.

of the risen Christ with that of the life-giving Spirit.[78] Here, in this last point, we can see Paul's christology doing something similar to what it did also with Wisdom—Christ as absorbing the Spirit's life-giving role. The difference is that it was only with Christ's exaltation that this happened, not in a concept of incarnation.

We could press the thought a little further. For Paul's language seems to imply that for Paul experience of the Spirit was experience of Christ.[79] So we could say that, for Paul, as the Spirit had hitherto mediated the presence of God, and as Jesus in his life had mediated the presence of God, so now the Spirit also mediated the presence of Christ. But this implies that for Paul the Spirit now related to Christ in the same way that the Spirit had always related to God – as the medium of divine presence. This implies in turn that both the exalted Jesus and the Spirit were bound up in the same divine presence.[80]

Could we infer, should we infer, that Paul thought it necessary to maintain a distinction between the exalted Christ and the divine Spirit understood as given to and active within humankind? This, even though he also sometimes spoke of Christ as indwelling believers,[81] as the Spirit indwells believers.[82] The Spirit remained the primary way of speaking of the divine presence within, whereas Jesus was most regularly thought of as exalted at God's right hand – much as the Johannine literature was subsequently to speak of the Spirit as the Paraclete/Advocate on earth and Christ as the Paraclete/Advocate in

---

[78] Fatehi seems to struggle to avoid this conclusion (*The Spirit's Relation to the Risen Lord* 285–6 – 'a life-giving *pneuma*'), but accepts it in the end (286–8, 302–3 – 'Paul does identify the Spirit with the risen Christ').

[79] See my *Jesus and the Spirit* (London: SCM Press, 1975) 322–4.

[80] Fatehi does press the point: Paul's Spirit-language 'points in the direction of the concept of God itself in a way that it would include Christ. No divine agent or mediatorial being merely *alongside* God and *separate* from him could possibly be thought of as being present and active through God's Spirit' (*The Spirit's Relation to the Risen Lord* 326; and further 315–30).

[81] Rom. 8.10; 2 Cor. 13.5; Gal. 2.20; Col. 1.27.

[82] E.g. Rom. 8.9, 11; 1 Co. 3.16; 6.19.

heaven.[83] The point not to be neglected, however, is that Paul saw the roles as overlapping. If the Spirit was the pre-eminent and classical way of speaking of the divine life and presence within humankind, Christ could also be spoken of as bringing and constituting the divine presence within humankind, or as the divine presence within which believers had their being and found their *raison d'être* ('in Christ') – the Spirit as the Spirit of Christ, Christ as the life-giving Spirit. In other words, we are back into the mediatorial role of Christ – Christ not only as the way and means by which believers come to God, but the way in and as which God as Spirit enters into a life or human situation, Christ as embodying and defining the character of that divine presence.

What emerges consistently from this section is that the earliest Christians radically reinterpreted the language and imagery by which Israel's sages and theologians spoke of God's perceptible activity within human experience by filling it out by reference to Jesus. The creative energy of God, the moral character of the cosmos, the inspiration experienced by prophets, the saving purpose of God for his people all came to fuller/fullest expression in Christ. This did not mean that Jesus should be worshipped in himself, any more than the Word as such, divine Wisdom as such or the Spirit of God as such was or should have been worshipped. But it did mean that as the divine self-revelation, through Spirit, Wisdom and Word, more fully informed and enabled worship of the one God, the same was even more the case with Christ. As early as the first Christians, it was recognized that the one God should be worshipped as the God active in and through Jesus, indeed, in a real sense as Jesus – Jesus as the clearest self-revelation of the one God ever given to humankind. As the opening words of Hebrews put it: whereas God had spoken to previous generations in many and various ways by the prophets, now 'in these last days he has spoken by a Son . . . the radiance of God's glory and the stamp of his nature' (Heb. 1.1–3).

---

[83] John 14.16, 26; 15.26; 16.7; 1 John 2.1.

4.4 The testimony of the Apocalypse of John

The book of Revelation deserves separate treatment on this subject, for it is unique among the New Testament documents. It is unique not simply as the only apocalypse to have gained a place in the New Testament. It is unique because unlike the other main writings in the New Testament its affirmation of the deity of Christ is unqualified. Paul we noted on the whole refrains from using worship language in reference to Christ, and though he speaks of the divine Lordship of Christ he also speaks of God as the God of the Lord Jesus Christ. Hebrews affirms Jesus' role and status uninhibitedly as the Wisdom of God, but it also speaks of Jesus as having to learn obedience and to be perfected through his suffering. Even John's Gospel, which does not hesitate to use the term *theos*, 'god', for the Word, and indeed for the Word become flesh, also speaks of Jesus not simply as the Word, but as the Word become flesh; and the Johannine letters portray Jesus as still praying to the Father, now that he is in heaven (1 John 2.1). In the Apocalypse of John, however, all such restraint has gone, beyond the fact that Christ is represented as the Lamb that had been slaughtered.

The uninhibitedness of Revelation's christology is easily illustrated:[84]

- Its vision of Jesus as the Son of Man (Rev. 1.12–16) mingles the imagery of the man-like figure who takes a throne beside the Ancient of Days (Dan. 7.13) with the description used of the Ancient of Days himself (7.9) and of the One who sat on the chariot throne in Ezekiel 1.24–27.
- Both the Lord God and soon-coming Christ say the same words, 'I am the Alpha and the Omega', the first and the last, the beginning and the end (1.8; 22.13).

---

[84] More fully in *The Partings of the Ways* #11.4. 'The presentation of Jesus' exalted status in Revelation is unexcelled among first-century Christian texts' (Hurtado, *Lord Jesus Christ* 594).

- The worship of the Lamb in Chapter 5 is no different in character as worship from the worship of the Lord God Almighty in Chapter 4; the 'living creatures' and the 24 elders 'worship' (*proskynein*) in both cases (4.9–11; 5.13–14). Worship that once again is denied as applicable even to glorious angels (19.10) is entirely appropriate to the Lamb.
- In his visions the seer no longer makes a point of distinguishing the throne of the Lamb from that of God. Some of the descriptions seem to imply that the Lamb is seen to be sitting on *God's* throne (7.17), and 22.1, 3 speak of 'the throne [singular] of God and of the Lamb'.[85]
- The imagery of first-fruits is envisaged as offered to both God and the Lamb (14.4), and those who share in the first resurrection 'will be priests of God and of Christ' (20.6).

Now such unique lack of inhibition can be explained in part at least by the uniqueness of the book of Revelation as the only New Testament apocalypse. Apocalyptic visions major on the grandiose and the bizarre, on startling symbolism and hyperbole. The status given to or recognized for the Lamb has to be read in the context of the cosmic evil portrayed in the images of the great dragon, the horrific beast and the richly clad prostitute. That is not the language of everyday theology nor the context of everyday worship. Apocalyptic visions burst free from such constraints and portray their message in the symbolism, often grotesque symbolism, of a Hieronymus Bosch. The exaggerated lines of the brightly coloured depictions are a way of figuring a reality that is beyond everyday description and imagery. Even so, the status attributed to and recognized for the exalted

---

[85] It is in Revelation's merger (in effect) of the two thrones implied in Ps. 110.1 into one throne that we probably come closest to Bauckham's understanding of the exalted Jesus being included in the divine identity (*God Crucified* 62–3 = *Jesus and the God of Israel* 45–6) – though he also observes that in Second Temple Jewish literature Wisdom is represented as sharing God's throne (*1 Enoch* 84.2–3; Wisd. 9.4, 10) and that 'in the Parables of Enoch, it is not on a second throne but on the single divine throne that the Son of Man takes his seat for eschatological judgment' and accordingly is worshipped (*1 Enoch* 48.5) (*Jesus and the God of Israel* 162, 165–6, 169–72).

Christ (the Lamb) should not be played down. The merging of the Son of Man with the Ancient of Days and of the Lamb with the Lord God are to be taken with the same seriousness as the high christologies of the other New Testament writers. The question posed, however, is whether the visions of the seer of Revelation are more like a highly coloured symbolical assertion of what he indeed shared with the other christologies just reviewed (the Lord Christ as the divine presence), than the description of a reality that can be expressed in literal terms and propositions. Is the imagery perhaps better described as surreal than as real metaphysics? The hermeneutical rule governing the interpretation of apocalypses should not be forgotten: to interpret them literally is to misinterpret them.

4.5 Jesus as god/God

In some ways this is the most difficult issue: that in the New Testament Jesus is sometimes called 'god', or should we say 'God'? If 'god', is not that a step towards polytheism – Jesus as a second god beside the creator God? If 'God', then how are we to make sense of the first Christians' clear memory that Jesus called for worship to be given only to God, and himself regularly prayed to God as his God and Father? The data itself poses as many questions as it resolves.

Did the first Christians think of Jesus as god/God? If Paul is the clearest, perhaps the only, spokesman for the first generation of Christians still available to us, the question draws our attention to Romans 9.5.[86] On syntactical grounds a strong case can be made for reading the text as a doxology to Christ as God:

> ... from whom [Israel] is the Christ according to the flesh, he who is over all, God blessed for ever.

And a good many commentators on Romans take this to have been Paul's intention – to pronounce a doxology to Jesus as

---

[86] See *Theology of Paul* 255–7, with further bibliography.

God. But the punctuation, which was not indicated in the original letter, can be arranged differently:

> . . . the Christ according to the flesh. He who is over all, God, may he be blessed for ever.

And there is more to be said for this latter reading than is often appreciated. Above all there is the fact that the passage is a catalogue of Israel's privileges, where it is likely that Paul was enumerating the blessings that Israel claimed for itself and in the language that Israel would recognize and affirm – 'to them [Israelites] belong the adoption, the glory, the covenants, the giving of the law, the worship and the promises . . . the patriarchs and . . . the Messiah'. It would be entirely fitting after such a listing of God's goodness towards Israel to utter a doxology in praise of this God, rather as Paul does in Romans 1.25 and 11.33–36. So it remains finally unclear and open to question as to whether Paul here, exceptionally for him, spoke of Jesus as god/God.

A stronger case is Titus 2.13, which speaks of 'the appearing of the glory of our great God and Saviour Jesus Christ'. To be noted, however, is that the 'appearing' (*epiphaneia*) in view is the appearing of the divine *glory*, not the appearing of Jesus Christ in glory. This may seem a small point, but it may also signify that we are back in the thought most clearly expressed in earliest Christianity's Wisdom christology: that in Jesus is to be seen the glory of God, the glory of the divine presence;[87] Jesus Christ seen more as the visible manifestation of the invisible God, God manifesting himself in and through Jesus, than as God or a god as such. The fact that the Pastoral Epistles seem to be content to attribute the title 'Saviour' equally (and we might almost say, indiscriminately) to 'our God'[88] as to Christ Jesus,[89] probably points in the same direction: Jesus' death and life were to be seen as the saving action of God.

---

[87] As also in John 1.18 and 12.41.

[88] 1 Tim. 1.1; 2.3; 4.10; Titus 1.3; 2.10; 3.4.

[89] 2 Tim. 1.10; Titus 1.4; 2.13; 3.6.

In Matthew's Gospel we should note the strong strand of divine presence.[90] Jesus is to be named 'Emmanuel, God with us' (Matt. 1.23), though we should recall that the passage quoted (Isa. 7.14) looked for the not too distant birth of an unknown child who was to be given the symbolical name Emmanuel. Matthew has taken seriously its application and appropriateness to Jesus by showing Jesus as promising to be present where even only two or three are gathered in his name (18.20) and the risen Jesus as promising to be with his disciples 'always, to the end of the age' (28.20). This is nothing other than a promise that the divine presence will be with Jesus' disciples, wherever they gather in his name, and for evermore. Which is also to say that Jesus himself constitutes that divine presence – as he did already in his life and mission, so he continues to do in his resurrection and exaltation.

We have already noted the attribution of the title 'God'/'god' to Jesus in John's Gospel – the pre-incarnate Word as God (John 1.1), the incarnate Word as the only begotten God/god who makes known the unseen/unseeable God (1.18), and the risen Christ worshipped as 'my Lord and my God' by Thomas (20.28). The fact that even when describing the Logos as God/god (1.1), John may distinguish two uses of the title from each other is often noted but too little appreciated. The distinction is possibly made by the use of the definite article with *theos* and the absence of the definite article in the same sentence: 'In the beginning was the *logos* and the *logos* was with God (literally, the God, *ton theon*), and the *logos* was god/God (*theos*, without the definite article).'[91] Such a distinction may have been

---

[90] See particularly D. Kupp, *Matthew's Emmanuel: Divine Presence and God's People in the First Gospel* (SNTSMS 90; Cambridge: Cambridge University Press, 1996).

[91] Grammatically the absence of the definite article may simply indicate that *theos*, though preceding the verb, is the predicate and not the subject; see J. H. Moulton and N. Turner, *A Grammar of New Testament Greek*, Vol. III (Edinburgh: T&T Clark, 1963) 183–4. Unfortunately the rule does not enable us to say whether the definite article was intended, and whether the hearer/reader was intended to assume its presence (no distinction between *ho theos* and *theos*). In John 20.28 the article is used, but its absence in 1.1c may reinforce the hesitation about identifying the pre-incarnate Logos *tout simple* with Jesus.

intended, since the absence or presence of the article with *theos* was a matter of some sensitivity. As we see in Philo, in his exposition of Genesis 31.13 (*De Somniis* 1.227–30):

> He that is truly God is One, but those who are improperly so called are more than one. Accordingly the holy word in the present instance has indicated him who is truly God by means of the article, saying 'I am the God', while it omits the article when mentioning him who is improperly so called, saying, 'Who appeared to thee in the place' not 'of the God', but simply 'of God' [Gen. 31.13]. Here it gives the title of 'God' to his chief Word.

The possible parallel is notable, since Philo was clearly willing to speak of the Logos as 'God', as we see here and already noted in Chapter 3. But he did so in clear awareness that in so doing he was speaking only of God's outreach to humankind in and through and as the Logos, not of God in himself. John's Gospel does not attempt similar clarification in his use of God/god for the Logos, pre-incarnate and incarnate, though he uses language in regard to Christ that is very close to that of Philo in regard to the Logos.[92] But in possibly making (or allowing to be read) a distinction between God (*ho theos*) and the Logos (*theos*) the Evangelist may have had in mind a similar qualification in the divine status to be recognized for Christ. Jesus was God, in that he made God known, in that God made himself known in and through him, in that he was God's effective outreach to his creation and to his people. But he was not God in himself.[93] There was more to God than God had manifested in and through his incarnate Word.

The same is probably true of the other important Johannine text here – 1 John 5.19–20. For the passage expresses gratitude

---

[92] As noted in Ch. 3.3(c), Philo speaks of the Logos both as God's 'firstborn son' (*Agr.* 51), and as 'the second God' (*Qu. Gen.* 2.62).

[93] Hence, presumably, John had no qualms in depicting Jesus as defending himself against the charge that he was making himself God by citing the fact that Ps. 82.6 called other human beings 'gods' (John 10.33–35). See also McHugh, *John 1–4* 10.

for the understanding that the Son of God has given us 'so that we may know him who is true [presumably God], and we are in him who is true, in his Son Jesus Christ. He is the true God and eternal life.' If the last 'he' refers to Jesus (though the point is unclear and disputed), then as with John's Gospel, the godness of Jesus Christ is that as God's Son he fully represents God; to be in Christ is to be in God, or to be in him is to know God; the Son has made God known and present. As such he can even be described as 'the true God and eternal life'. It is because the depth and profundity of God has been so fully revealed in and through Christ that Christ can be described as the revelation of the true God.

Since we have already given some attention to the Revelation of John, the only other text that needs to be taken into account here is Hebrews. For in Hebrews 1.8 the writer quotes Psalm 45.6 as an address to the Son: 'Your throne, O God, is for ever and ever.' Following the strong Wisdom christology of the opening verses (1.1–4), and the interpretation of Deuteronomy 32.43 as a call on the angels to worship God's firstborn Son (1.6), the text must be given due weight. At the same time, however, we should recall that Psalm 45.6–7 was probably addressed to Israel's king, a fact that the writer of Hebrews was probably aware of since he carries on the quotation to Psalm 45.7, which speaks of the king as having been anointed by 'God, your God'. So again we are confronted with the use of 'God'/'god' in a transferred sense, emphasizing the divinely accorded status of an individual while always aware that God was still the God of the one so described. In effect we are back into the powerful significance that Paul saw in Jesus' Lordship while he continued to think of God as the God of the Lord Jesus Christ.

4.6 Last Adam, mediator, heavenly intercessor

Although our focus is naturally on the high christology of the heavenly or divine status of Jesus, before we close this chapter we should recall the fuller roundedness of the New Testament christologies. We have noted at various points how the understanding of Jesus as the one who brings God close to the human condition is balanced (is that the right word?) by the understanding of Jesus as the one who brings humankind close to God. The traditional attempt to capture this fuller portrayal has been to emphasize the human as well as the divine in Jesus. But the distinction is too crude, already for the New Testament writers.

(a) Last Adam

An important, though controversial aspect of Paul's christology is his depiction of Christ as the last, or second, Adam. This is most explicit in Romans 5.12–19, 7.7–13 and 1 Corinthians 15.21–22, 45, but is probably alluded to or drawn on elsewhere.[94] The message is clear: the first Adam (man) had failed by his disobedience; the last Adam had reversed, and more than reversed the failure. The implication is clear too: that in Christ, the last Adam, God's purpose in creating Adam/man had been fulfilled. Christ, that is the Christ who died and has been resurrected, provides the pattern for God's saving purpose. He is the firstborn among many brothers (Rom. 8.29; Heb. 12.23); those who pray 'Abba, Father' thus share in Jesus' sonship (Rom. 8.15–17; Gal. 4.6–7). He is the firstborn from the dead (Col. 1.18; Rev. 1.5), the beginning of the new creation. As (the last) Adam, Christ represents humankind before God. This is

---

[94] Rom. 1.19–23; 3.23; 8.20–21; Phil. 2.6–11; see *Theology of Paul* 90–101. Bauckham thinks that 'Adam has proved a red herring' in the study of Phil. 2.6–11 (*God Crucified* 57 = *Jesus and the God of Israel* 41; also 203, 207–8). And Hurtado thinks I attribute too much to a supposed 'Adam Christology' in Paul's letters (*Lord Jesus Christ* 121 n. 98; also *How on Earth* 98–101), though to play down an allusion to the temptation to 'be like God' (Gen. 3.5) because the temptation was actually made to Eve (*How on Earth* 100; similarly Fee, *Pauline Christology* 390–3) treats the character of an 'allusion' too woodenly (see my *Theology of Paul* 283–4). One should allow the possibility that the story of Jesus was being shaped to the template of the Adam story, the one who, acting differently from Adam, yet submitted to death like Adam, and thus far outdid Adam's failure and tragedy (cf. Rom. 5.12–19). Like other templates (e.g. Christ as Word and Wisdom, priest and sacrifice, intercessor and mediator, eldest brother and forerunner, foundation and cornerstone) the template should not be treated as a rigid frame that imprisons the meaning of the story (the parable of the prodigal son has no place for Jesus), but as a suggestive parallel that allows the story to be seen from a different angle.

an important qualification beside Christ's role in representing God to humankind. The point comes to expression in various ways, each indicating that the two-sidedness of Jesus' role between God and humankind was important.

It comes to expression in the language of 'image' (*eikōn*). For the term can be used both of Adam, created in God's image (Gen. 1.27), and of the divine Wisdom through whom God creates (Wisd. 7.26; Col. 1.15; cf. 2 Cor. 4.4). The stamp leaves its impression on the wax that is stamped, and *eikōn* can be used of both. This two-sidedness of Jesus' role in the purpose of God remains important. Christ is the image to which his fellow brothers will be conformed (Rom. 8.29); his is the image into which they are being transformed (2 Cor. 3.18). But the claim can equally well be made of a renewal in accordance with the image of its creator (Col. 3.10). Here again the implication is that the saving purpose of God is to bring to full effect his creative purpose; the last Adam is the divine image, the pattern to which all will be conformed (1 Cor. 15.49).

In the same connection, one of the intriguing features of the earliest Christian reflection on Psalm 110.1 was the way it was merged in their thinking with Psalm 8.6. Psalm 110.1 spoke of the Lord God seating the Psalmist's Lord at his right hand 'until I make your enemies a footstool for your feet'. But the earliest Christian reflection on Psalm 110.1 evidently saw a link with the description in Psalm 8 of God's purpose in making humankind, itself a meditation on the second account of creation in Genesis 2.19–20:

> You have made them a little lower than God/the angels (*elohim*),
> and crowned them with glory and honour.
> You have given them dominion over the work of your hands;
> you have put all things under their feet.
>
> (Ps. 8.5–6, NRSV, adapted)

Psalm 8's talk of God having 'put all things under [humankind's/Adam's] feet' was evidently too close to Psalm 110's talk of Yahweh making his enemies a footstool for the Lord Christ's feet to be ignored. So what we find is that either Psalm 8.6b is drawn in to complement Psalm 110.1 (as in 1 Cor. 15.25–27),[95] or the citation of Psalm 110.1 is modified by incorporating the phrasing of Psalm 8.6.[96] Presumably the implication, for those who understood Psalm 110.1 in terms of Psalm 8.6, was that the exaltation of *Christ* to the right hand of God was also the ultimate fulfilment of God's purpose for *humankind* in creation. Here surprisingly, given the weight of the former, *kyrios* christology seems to overlap in earliest christology with what is usually described as Paul's Adam christology. In other words, the readiness to apply Yahweh texts to the exalted Christ was complemented by the affirmation that Christ's exaltation to God's right hand also fulfilled the divine purpose for human-kind intended from the very act of creation.

Hebrews is one of the best examples of a New Testament writing that tries to maintain this balance. For the climactic revelation through the Son (Heb. 1.1–4) can also be expressed (again) in the divine purpose for humankind fulfilled now in Christ, drawing directly on Psalm 8.4–6 (Heb. 2.6–9), and in terms of the Son who 'learned obedience through what he suffered' and who had to be 'made perfect' in order to become 'the source of eternal salvation' (5.7–9).[97] The same point is presumably in mind in Hebrews' repeated description of Jesus as '*mediator* of a new covenant'.[98] And it may not be accidental that it is 1 Timothy, the member of the Pauline corpus that seems to go most out of its way to repeatedly affirm its strong monotheistic standpoint,[99] which also declares the 'one

---

[95] Also Eph. 1.20–22 and Heb. 1.3—2.8.

[96] Mark. 12.36/Matt. 22.44; 1 Pet. 3.22. 'Under your feet' (Ps. 8.6) was presumably taken to be synonymous with 'a footstool for your feet' (Ps. 110.1). For more detail see Hengel, '"Sit at My Right Hand"' 163–71.

[97] R. Bauckham, 'Monotheism and Christology in Hebrews 1', in Stuckenbruck and North (eds), *Early Jewish and Christian Monotheism* 167–85, finds in this two-fold emphasis in Hebrews a foreshadowing of the two-natures christology of Chalcedon (185).

[98] Heb. 8.6; 9.15; 12.24.

[99] 1 Tim. 1.17 ('the only God'); 2.5 ('one God'); 6.15–16 ('the only Sovereign . . . he alone who has immortality and dwells in unapproachable light, whom no one has ever seen or can see').

mediator between God and humankind' to be 'the man Christ Jesus' (1 Tim. 2.5). The 'one God, one Lord' formula of 1 Corinthians 8.6, is now, or is alternatively expressed as, 'one God, one mediator'.

(b) Heavenly intercessor

In examining the striking features of the New Testament's high christology, we should not forget that another strand, also drawing on the thought of Christ's exaltation, sees Jesus as the one who intercedes for humans. This strand runs across an interesting spectrum of the New Testament. In the great climax to his exposition in Romans 8, Paul is confident that in the final judgment Christ Jesus will be at the right hand of God as the one who 'intercedes for us' (8.34). Since the motif of angelic intercessors was already familiar within Second Temple Judaism,[100] the implication is that Paul saw the intercession of God's own Son, who had died and been raised, as decisive, and thus presumably as much more powerful than that of even glorious angels. 1 John 2.1 likewise counsels encouragement: 'If anyone does sin, we have an advocate with the Father, Jesus Christ the righteous.' Here, as already noted, the assumption is that not only is the Holy Spirit the advocate (*paraklētos*) on earth,[101] but Christ fulfils the same role in heaven, once again all the more effective in that he pleads his own 'atoning sacrifice' (1 John 2.2).

But once again it is Hebrews that makes the most of the thought of Jesus as the heavenly intercessor.[102] This is an integral part of Hebrews' conception of Christ as High Priest: Christ is not like earthly priests, whose office ends with death; rather, Christ

---

[100] E.g. Job 33.23–26; Tobit 12.15; *1 Enoch* 9.3; 15.2; 99.3; 104.1; *T. Levi* 3.5; 5.6–7; *T. Dan* 6.2.

[101] John 14.16, 26; 15.26; 16.7; cf. Rom. 8.27.

[102] As Bauckham noted (Ch. 3 n. 30), *Apoc. Ab.* seems to regard the angel Yahoel as 'the heavenly high priest'.

holds his priesthood permanently, because he continues for ever. Consequently he is able for all time to save those who approach God through him, since he always lives to make intercession for them. (Heb. 7.24–25, NRSV)

It is this function of priestly office, the priest as intermediary between God and humans, that Hebrews emphasizes so much. Precisely as one who knows and has experienced the weaknesses of human beings, who has 'learned obedience through what he suffered', Christ can empathize with and help those who come to God through him.[103] This is an important other side to the question of whether Jesus was prayed to by the first Christians. Equally, indeed more, important for many of these Christians was the assurance that Jesus was praying *for* them. Here again we find ourselves with the two-sidedness of the first Christians' esteem for Christ, both as the mediator between God and man, the one through whom they could come confidently to God, and as the one who was also conjoint with God in the worship they brought to God.

4.7 How helpful is it to re-express the issues in terms of 'divine identity'?

As noted at the beginning of Chapter 3, Bauckham argues that it does most justice to the New Testament texts and to the christology espoused by the first Christians to see them as identifying Jesus directly with the one God of Israel. In the light of our findings, it is appropriate to ask whether this new coinage of 'divine identity', and Bauckham's thesis that the first Christians saw Jesus as sharing or included in the divine identity, is a helpful resolution to the tensions between the diverse ways in which Paul and the first Christians conceptualized the relationship of Jesus to God and to themselves. Bauckham offers this formula as a more satisfactory alternative to the standard distinction between a 'functional' and an 'ontic'

---

[103] Heb. 2.17–18; 4.15–16; 6.7–10, 19–20; 10.19–22; 12.24.

christology, as providing a more satisfactory way of assessing the earliest christological reflection, within the matrix and traditions of Second Temple Judaism, than exploration of its concepts of divine agents and heavenly intermediaries. And certainly talk of 'sharing the divine identity' is a way of taking seriously and doing justice to the emphasis in the New Testament writings that I sum up in the previous paragraphs as Jesus seen to embody the divine presence. But I have some reservations.

The first concerns the value of 'identity' as the key structural term. It seems to me to run the danger of confusing rather than clarifying. The traditional term of classic christology, 'person', has long been recognized as caught in precisely that danger, since the usual present-day understanding of 'person' is so different from the technical understanding of *persona*, which was the term that was drawn in to provide a way of distinguishing Father, Son and Spirit within the Trinity.[104] 'Identity' runs the same risk. What constitutes human/personal identity? Ethnic origin, country of birth and basic education, profession, family (parents, children, siblings, extended family), colleagues, friends, hobbies . . .? If not 'essence' or 'being', then relationships. So how does that diversity in identity-composition work in relation to Yahweh – the Creator, the Life-giver, the God of Israel, the Father and God of the Lord Jesus Christ, the final Judge . . .? The New Testament writers are really quite careful at this point. Jesus is not the God of Israel. He is not the Father. He is not Yahweh. An identification of Jesus with and as Yahweh was an early attempt to resolve the tensions indicated above; it was labelled as 'Modalism', a form of 'Monarchianism' (the one God operating first as Father and then as Son), and accounted a heresy.[105] My question, then, is whether talk of 'sharing divine

---

[104] As noted at the beginning (Introduction n. 1). The Latin *persona* denoted basically a 'mask', especially as used by actors in a play, which represented the character being played; and so by extension it came to denote the 'character' itself (*ALD* 1355–6).

[105] See e.g. *ODCC* 1102; J. N. D. Kelly, *Early Christian Doctrine* (London: A. & C. Black, ²1960) 115–23.

identity' does enough justice to the history of Jesus and to the diverse roles attributed to Jesus that are distinguished from God's.

My second reservation follows from the first. For classic christology has always seen the need to affirm a paradoxical 'both–and', summed up in the traditional confession of Jesus as having both a divine and a human nature. The distinction between 'functional' and 'ontic' is a more modern attempt to hold together, however unsatisfactorily, the same two divergent or apparently contradictory sets of data, as summarized above. The language of 'divine agency' and 'plenipotentiary' are similarly attempts to hold together what seem to pull apart from each other. This is where, I still maintain, the early Jewish reflection about divine Wisdom and Word continues to provide important precedents for what the first Christians were trying to say about Jesus – that he embodied God's immanence, that he was the visible image of the invisible God, that he was as full an expression of God's creative and redemptive concern and action as was possible in flesh. Certainly embodying God's 'identity' as embodying the creative and redemptive purpose and energy of God. But 'function' or 'agency' also expresses the point and without the confusion that would otherwise lead us to speak of partial identity.[106] How different is it to affirm that the first Christians saw Jesus as included in the divine identity from affirming that they saw Jesus as exercising divine functions? So I remain unclear as to the advantages that introducing 'divine identity' as the key term produces, and I remain concerned as to the dimensions and aspects of New Testament christology that the term 'identity' pushes to the side.

One of the problems with Bauckham's formulation, his enthusiasm for and insistence on it, is that he uses it in a way that may not unfairly be described as indiscriminate. If God's unique role is as Creator, both source (*ek*) and agent (*dia*), as

---

[106] McGrath argues that 'divine agency' does more justice to the range of statements made about Jesus by the fourth evangelist, including the latter's prominent 'sent' motif (*The Only True God* 118 n. 8; 119 n. 10).

143

in Romans 11.36, then Jesus shares in that role as divine agent (*dia*) but not as source (*ek*).[107] The identity is partial. If the uniqueness of God is that he is 'the sole sovereign Ruler of all things', then according to 1 Corinthians 15.24–28, Jesus as God's Son shares that role as the one who sits at God's right hand (all things subjected to him), but in the end 'the Son himself will be subjected to the one who subjected all things to him, in order that God might be [the] all in all' (15.28). If the uniqueness of God is that he is the God of Israel, then Jesus shares in that identity in a derivative way, as the one promised by the covenant God to be Israel's Messiah. My concern with Bauckham's thesis, then, is that by pushing so much through the narrow-holed sieve of 'divine identity', he may be squeezing out the rich diversity of allusion and the range of surplus meaning in the variety of images and language that the New Testament writers evidently felt both desirable and necessary to use in talking about Jesus and their reverence for Jesus.

Given the degree of confusion that 'identity' seems to involve, would 'equation' be a better term than 'identity'? The mathematical distinction between the two terms may be helpful here: that is the distinction between 'A equals B' and 'A is identical with B'. The equation formula means that for some values of A and/or some values of B, A and B are the same. The identity formula means that for *all* values of A and for *all* values of B, A and B are the same; A and B are never different or distinct from each other. 'Equation' seems to be a better way of saying that if Jesus is God he is not YHWH, he is not the Father, he is not the source of creation, he will finally be subject to God so that God (alone) will be all in all. 'Equation' allows a fuller recognition of the other emphases in the New Testament writings – Jesus as Jesus of Nazareth praying to God, Jesus as last Adam and eldest brother in God's new creation family, Jesus as heavenly intercessor, God as God of the Lord Jesus Christ.

---

[107] This, partly in response to Bauckham, *Jesus and the God of Israel* 213–17.

4.8 Conclusion

The results of this survey are astonishing. Here was the man Jesus of Nazareth, who had been executed within the lifetime of most of those who wrote the New Testament writings. He had made a huge impact as a prophet and exceptional teacher during his mission. He was regarded by his followers as the Messiah that Israel had longed for. But they were also convinced that in him the resurrection expected at the end of the age had already happened. They were convinced that God had exalted him to his right hand. They saw him as their Lord and did not hesitate to ascribe to him as Lord what various scriptures had ascribed only to the Lord God. They called upon his name in invocation and prayer. The roles that Israel's sages and theologians had ascribed to Wisdom and God's Word, they ascribed to him, even the latters' role as the divine agents of creation; in Christ the personification became the person. They ascribed to him the outpouring of the Spirit and the Spirit's life-giving power. The seer of Revelation saw visions of universal worship being given to the Lamb. The title or status of God/god was used for him.

Yet at the same time they recalled that this was Jesus of Nazareth, who affirmed the same monotheistic creed as they did, who forbad worship of any other than God, and who prayed to God as an expression of his own need of and reliance on God. They saw that the exalted Jesus was the mediator through whom they approached God, the one in whose name and through whom they gave thanks and glory to God, the one who at God's right hand interceded for them. They recognized that God was still Jesus' God, even the God of Jesus as Lord. Their use of Wisdom and Logos imagery was probably intended as an extension and creative reworking of the vivid imagery used by Israel's sages and theologians, a 'mutation' in Hurtado's words. Similarly their use of *theos* in relation to Jesus was probably with a similar qualification that there was much more to God than could be seen in and through Jesus. In short, Jesus was Last Adam as well as Lord, mediator as well as Saviour, the one who prayed for them as well as the one whose name they invoked.

But the findings are not adequately summed up in just these two apparently diverging lists. For the dominant impression that comes through is that Jesus was understood to embody the outreach of God himself, that Jesus was in a real sense God reaching out to humankind; that, as Lord, Jesus shared fully in the one Lordship of God; that, like Wisdom/Word and as Wisdom/Word, he was to be seen as God making himself known to his own; that the Spirit of God was now to be recognized as being defined more as the Spirit of Christ. As in the first two chapters we began to see that, for the first Christians, Christ was the means and the way by which they could come to God, so now the impression grows ever stronger that they also saw Christ as the means and the way by which God has come most effectively to humankind. Jesus as mediator mediated in both directions, not only to God but also from God. Jesus summed up and embodied for them the divine presence.[108]

So when we transpose our findings into an answer to our central question, the dominant answer for Christian worship seems to be that the first Christians did not think of Jesus as to be worshipped in and for himself. He was not to be worshipped as wholly God, or fully identified with God, far less as a god. If he was worshipped it was worship offered to God in and through him, worship of Jesus-in-God and God-in-Jesus. And the corollary is that, in an important sense, Christian monotheism, if it is to be truly monotheism, has still to assert that only God, only the one God, is to be worshipped. The Christian distinctive within the monotheistic faiths is its affirmation that God is most effectively worshipped in and through, and, in some real but finally unquantifiable sense, as (revealed in) Jesus.

---

[108] It remains a question whether 'divine agency' is adequate or sufficient to express the full weight of this emphasis, just as the question remains whether 'divine identity' is adequate or sufficient to sum up the full range of imagery and language used for Jesus in the NT.

Conclusion

The answer

This inquiry has clarified a number of important points that feed into the answer to its central question, 'Did the first Christians worship Jesus?'

One is that there are some problems, even dangers, in Christian worship if it is defined too simply as worship of Jesus. For, if what has emerged in this inquiry is taken seriously, it soon becomes evident that Christian worship can deteriorate into what may be called Jesus-olatry. That is, not simply into worship of Jesus, but into a worship that falls short of the worship due to the one God and Father of our Lord Jesus Christ. I use the term 'Jesus-olatry' as in an important sense parallel or even close to 'idolatry'. As Israel's prophets pointed out on several occasions, the calamity of idolatry is that the idol is in effect taken to be the god to be worshipped. So the idol substitutes for the god, takes the place of God. The worship due to God is absorbed by the idol. The danger of Jesus-olatry is similar: that Jesus has been substituted for God, has taken the place of the one creator God; Jesus is absorbing the worship due to God alone. It is this danger that helps explain why the New Testament refers to Jesus by the word 'icon' (*eikōn*) – the icon of the invisible God. For, as the lengthy debate in Eastern Christianity made clear, the distinction between an idol and an icon is crucial at this point. An *idol* is a depiction on which the eye fixes, a solid wall at which the worship stops. An *icon* on the other hand is a window through which the eye passes, through which the beyond can be seen, through which divine reality can be witnessed. So the danger with a worship that has become too predominantly the worship of Jesus is that the worship due to God is stopping at Jesus, and that the revelation of God through Jesus and the worship of God through Jesus is being stifled and short-circuited. It was because of such concerns that one of the leading figures and theologians of the early charismatic movement in the UK wrote a book entitled *The Forgotten Father.*[1] His warning still needs to be heeded.

To put it another way, there is a roundedness in the New Testament's evaluation of Jesus that the question, 'Did they worship Jesus?', can easily lose sight of. The Jesus whose name is invoked in prayer is also the Jesus who intercedes for his own. The Jesus who is Lord and the image of God is also the last Adam and pattern to whom believers are being conformed, the eldest brother in the family of the new creation. The Jesus through whom God has most clearly come to humankind is also the Jesus through whom worshippers come to God; he is the mediator.

A second point to be noted takes up the complementary issue of whether worship of Jesus constitutes a denial of Christianity's claim to be a monotheistic religion. As noted at the beginning of the Introduction, such a critique of Christian worship is made by the other great monotheistic faiths, Judaism and Islam. But it has become increasingly clear from the inquiry that the understanding of God as one, of the unity of God, is not so readily defined as such critiques generally assume. The unity or oneness of God is not a straightforward mathematical unity. Only a little acquaintance with mathematics, from ancient times until the present, will be sufficient to remind us that the concept of 'number' is more complex than at first seems likely, once we move on from merely counting apples and oranges or pennies and cents. We should recall, for example, that when Paul talks of the body of Christ, he insists that the body is one, the body

---

[1] T. A. Smail, *The Forgotten Father* (London: Hodder & Stoughton, 1980): 'There is a Jesuology that can lavish an all too human love on an all too human Jesus and banish God to such remote transcendence, that we are back with the idea that we have to cling to a loving Jesus to keep us right with a remote and probably angry God . . . To pray *to* Jesus rather than *through* him, *to* the Spirit rather than *in* him, as the established habit of our prayer, is to betray a doubt about our relationship to the Father' (169). Hurtado expresses similar concerns regarding worship that confuses God and Jesus (*Origins* 103–6); he concludes, 'Worship of Jesus properly is worship of the one God, through, and revealed in a unique way in, Jesus Christ' (118).

is a unity, but he insists equally that the one body is made up of many diverse members. Oneness is not necessarily an entity singular in all the elements that make it one, that form its oneness. Alternatively, a singular entity may be too big or complex (the cosmos) to be fully comprehended in its singularity. All that can be perceived are different aspects, aspects that do not easily cohere into one (in fundamental physics no one has yet been able to produce a unified field theory); but the inadequacies of human conceptualization do not constitute a denial of the singularity of the entity. So too, the oneness of God should not be assumed to be a narrowly defined mathematical unity. From earliest days in Israel's conceptuality of the oneness of God there was also recognized a diversity in the way God has been perceived or has made himself known. The one God made himself known in or through angelic form, as Spirit, as Wisdom, as Word, without detracting from his otherness, his transcendence, his being as the one and only God. So definitions of monotheism, of God's oneness, should not be so tightly drawn as to exclude such Hebrew Bible/Old Testament and early Jewish reflection on the subject. And Christianity can make the case that its evaluation of Jesus begins with that reflection and develops from it, but does so without calling in question that monotheism whose complex reality such reflection was attempting to articulate, however inadequately, and however open to misinterpretation of the monotheism espoused.[2]

A third point that has emerged is that Christian reflection on the significance and status of Jesus has been Christianity's principal attempt to make sense of how the gulf between the divine and the human is to be crossed. All religions are in their own ways attempts to affirm that the infinite gulf between

---

[2] It is somewhat curious that the question posed at the beginning focuses so exclusively on the worship of Jesus. It is not asked regarding the Holy Spirit, though one would have thought that, applying the same logic to a Trinitarian understanding of God, the same question could hardly be avoided. In fact the earliest instance we have of worship being rendered to the Holy Spirit alongside Christ and God is the *Ascension of Isaiah* (second century?); see Stuckenbruck, 'Worship and Monotheism in the *Ascension of Isaiah*' 78–82.

Creator and creation can be bridged and to show how that bridging takes place. In each case sacred places and sacred times, sacred liturgy and sacred ritual, sacred writings and sacred individuals (priest and lawgiver, prophet and sage), play critical roles. But Christianity has gone a step further in declaring that God has bridged the gulf not merely in scripture and temple, not only through priest and prophet, but in a particular individual through whom God revealed himself and who constitutes the bridge over the gulf in himself. That claim remains a claim too far for Jews and Muslims. But the claim that Christians make is that the character of God has never been revealed so fully and profoundly as in Jesus – in his mission, in his cruel death on the cross, and in his resurrection and exaltation. It is because Jesus died as he did that Christians find it necessary to speak of the God who suffers, even of 'the crucified God'. And so Christians feel able to speak also of a God who knows from within the weaknesses and temptations of the human condition and who can sustain both individuals and peoples in their various bewilderments and questionings, their tribulations and agonies. That conception of how the gulf is bridged has proved too controversial for other religions to embrace. But it is the contribution that Christianity offers to the resolution of the existential angst and conundrum that lie at the root of all religions. And Christians feel confident enough that God is as revealed most clearly in and through Jesus to commend this understanding of God to the wider religious world as the most profound insight into divine reality available to humankind.

In the light of such reflection and conclusion the particular question, 'Did the first Christians worship Jesus?', can be seen to be much less relevant, less important and potentially misleading. It can be answered simply, or simplistically, even dismissively, with a mainly negative answer. No, by and large the first Christians did not worship Jesus as such. Worship language and practice at times do appear in the New Testament in reference to Christ. But on the whole, there is more reserve on the subject. Christ is the subject of praise and hymn-singing, the content of early Christian worship, more than the one to whom the worship and praise is offered. More typical is the sense that the most (only?) effective worship, the most effective prayer is expressed in Christ and through Christ. That is also to say that we find a clear and variously articulated sense that Jesus enables worship – that Jesus is in a profound way the place and means of worship. Equally, it has become clear that for the first Christians Jesus was seen to be not only the one by whom believers come to God, but also the one by whom God has come to believers. The same sense of divine immanence in Spirit, Wisdom and Word was experienced also and more fully in and through Christ. He brought the divine presence into human experience more fully than had ever been the case before.

So our central question can indeed be answered negatively, and perhaps it should be. But not if the result is a far less adequate worship of God. For the worship that really constitutes Christianity and forms its distinctive contribution to the dialogue of the religions, is the worship of God as enabled by Jesus, the worship of God as revealed in and through Jesus. Christianity remains a monotheistic faith. The only one to be worshipped is the one God. But how can Christians fail to honour the one through whom it believes the only God has most fully revealed himself, the one through whom the only God has come closest to the condition of humankind? Jesus cannot fail to feature in their worship, their hymns of praise, their petitions to God. But such worship is always, should always be offered to the glory of God the Father. Such worship is always, should always be offered in the recognition that God is all in all, and that the majesty of the Lord Jesus in the end of the day expresses and affirms the majesty of the one God more clearly than anything else in the world.

Bibliography

Ådna, J., et al. (eds), *Evangelium – Schriftauslegung – Kirche*; P. Stuhlmacher FS (Göttingen: Vandenhoeck & Ruprecht, 1997)

Aschim, A., 'Melchizedek and Jesus: *11QMelchizedek* and the Epistle to the Hebrews', in C. C. Newman, et al. (eds), *The Jewish Roots of Christological Monotheism* 129–47

Aune, D. E., 'Worship, Early Christian', *ABD* 6.973–89

Barr, J., 'Abba Isn't Daddy!', *JTS* 39 (1988) 28–47

Barrett, C. K., *The First Epistle to the Corinthians* (London: A. & C. Black, 1968)

Bauckham, R. J., 'Biblical Theology and the Problem of Monotheism', in C. Bartholomew, et al. (eds), *Out of Egypt: Biblical Theology and Biblical Interpretation* (Milton Keynes: Paternoster, 2004) 187–232

Bauckham, R. J., *God Crucified: Monotheism and Christology in the New Testament* (Carlisle: Paternoster, 1998)

Bauckham, R. J., *Jesus and the God of Israel* (Milton Keynes: Paternoster, 2008)

Bauckham, R. J., 'Jesus, Worship of', *ABD* 3.812–19

Bauckham, R. J., *Jude, 2 Peter* (WBC 50; Waco: Word, 1983)

Bauckham, R. J., 'Monotheism and Christology in Hebrews 1', in L. T. Stuckenbruck and W. E. S. North (eds), *Early Jewish and Christian Monotheism* 167–85

Bauckham, R. J., 'Monotheism and Christology in the Gospel of John', in R. N. Longenecker (ed.), *Contours of Christology in the New Testament* (Grand Rapids: Eerdmans, 2005) 148–66

Bauckham, R. J., 'The Worship of Jesus in Apocalyptic Christianity', *NTS* 27 (1981) 322–41

Beegle, D. M., 'Moses', in D. N. Freedman (ed.), *Anchor Bible Dictionary* (6 vols; New York: Doubleday, 1992)

Botterweck, G. J., and Ringgren, H. (eds), *Theological Dictionary of the Old Testament* (ET; Grand Rapids: Eerdmans, 1974–2006)

Bousset, W., *Kyrios Christos* (1913, 1921; ET Nashville: Abingdon, 1970)

Bousset, W., and Gressmann, H., *Die Religion des Judentums im späthellenistischen Zeitalter* (HNT 22; Tübingen: Mohr Siebeck, 1925, [4]1966)

Box, G. H., 'The Idea of Intermediation in Jewish Theology', *JQR* 23 (1932–3) 103–19

Boyarin, D., *Border Lines: The Partition of Judaeo–Christianity* (Philadelphia: University of Pennsylvania Press, 2004)

Capes, D. B., *Old Testament Yahweh Texts in Paul's Christology* (WUNT 2.47; Tübingen: Mohr Siebeck, 1992)

Capes, D. B., 'ʏʜᴡʜ Texts and Monotheism in Paul's Christology', in L. T. Stuckenbruck and W. E. S. North (eds), *Early Jewish and Christian Monotheism* 120–37

Casey, P. M., *From Jewish Prophet to Gentile God: The Origins and Development of New Testament Christology* (Cambridge: James Clarke, 1991)

Casey, P. M., 'Monotheism, Worship and Christological Development in the Pauline Churches', in C. C. Newman, et al. (eds), *The Jewish Roots of Christological Monotheism* 214–33

Chester, A., *Messiah and Exaltation: Jewish Messianic and Visionary Traditions and New Testament Christology* (WUNT 207; Tübingen: Mohr Siebeck, 2007)

Cohon, S. S., 'The Unity of God: A Study in Hellenistic and Rabbinic Theology', *HUCA* 26 (1955) 425–79

Collins, A. Y., 'The Worship of Jesus and the Imperial Cult', in C. C. Newman, et al. (eds), *The Jewish Roots of Christological Monotheism* 234–57

Colson, F. H., *Philo* (LCL, 10 vols; Cambridge, MA: Harvard University Press, 1962)

Cullmann, O., *The Christology of the New Testament* (London: SCM Press, 1959)

Daly-Denton, M., 'Singing Hymns to Christ as to a God (cf. Pliny, *Ep.* X, 96)', in C. C. Newman, et al. (eds), *The Jewish Roots of Christological Monotheism* 277–92

Deichgräber, R., *Gotteshymnus und Christushymnus in der frühen Christenheit* (Göttingen: Vandenhoeck & Ruprecht, 1967)

Dunn, J. D. G., *Beginning From Jerusalem* (Grand Rapids: Eerdmans, 2009)

Dunn, J. D. G., *Christology in the Making: A New Testament Inquiry into the Origins of the Doctrine of the Incarnation* (London: SCM Press, 1980, ²1989; Grand Rapids: Eerdmans, 1996)

Dunn, J. D. G., *Colossians and Philemon* (NIGTC; Grand Rapids: Eerdmans, 1996)

Dunn, J. D. G., 'How Controversial was Paul's Christology?', in M. C. de Boer (ed.), *From Jesus to John: Essays on Jesus and New Testament*

Christology; M. de Jonge FS (JSNTS 84; Sheffield: JSOT, 1993)
148–67

Dunn, J. D. G., *Jesus and the Spirit: A Study of the Religious and Charismatic Experience of Jesus and the First Christians as Reflected in the New Testament* (London: SCM Press, 1975)

Dunn, J. D. G., *Jesus Remembered* (Grand Rapids: Eerdmans, 2003)

Dunn, J. D. G., 'KYRIOS in Acts', in C. Landmesser, et al., *Jesus Christus als die Mitte der Schrift*; Otfried Hofius FS; BZNW 86 (Berlin: de Gruyter, 1997)

Dunn, J. D. G., 'The Making of Christology – Evolution or Unfolding?', in J. B. Green and M. Turner (eds), *Jesus of Nazareth Lord and Christ*; I. H. Marshall FS (Grand Rapids: Eerdmans, 1994) 437–52

Dunn, J. D. G., *The Partings of the Ways between Christianity and Judaism* (London: SCM Press, 1991; [2]2006)

Dunn, J. D. G., 'Paul's Conversion – A Light to Twentieth Century Disputes', in E. Haenchen, *The Acts of the Apostles* (Oxford: Blackwell, 1971)

Dunn, J. D. G., *The Theology of Paul the Apostle* (Grand Rapids: Eerdmans/Edinburgh: T&T Clark, 1998)

Dunn, J. D. G., 'Was Jesus a Monotheist? A Contribution to the Discussion of Christian Monotheism', in L. T. Stuckenbruck and W. E. S. North (eds), *Early Jewish and Christian Monotheism* 104–19

Fatehi, M., *The Spirit's Relation to the Risen Lord in Paul: An Examination of its Christological Implications* (WUNT 2.128; Tübingen: Mohr Siebeck, 2000)

Fee, G. D., *Pauline Christology: An Exegetical–Theological Study* (Peabody: Hendrickson, 2007)

Finlan, S., and Kharlamov, V. (eds), *Theōsis: Deification in Christian Theology* (Eugene: Pickwick, 2006)

Fletcher-Louis, C. H. T., 'The Worship of Divine Humanity as God's Image and the Worship of Jesus', in C. C. Newman, et al. (eds), *The Jewish Roots of Christological Monotheism* 112–28

Haenchen, E., *The Acts of the Apostles* (Oxford: Blackwell, 1971)

Hayman, P., 'Monotheism – a Misused Word in Jewish Studies?', *JJS* 42 (1991) 1–15

Hayward, C. T. R., *The Jewish Temple: A Non-biblical Sourcebook* (London: Routledge, 1996)

Hengel, M., 'Hymns and Christology', *Between Jesus and Paul* (London: SCM Press, 1983) 78–96

Hengel, M., "'Sit at My Right Hand!'": The Enthronement of Christ at the Right Hand of God', *Studies in Early Christology* (Edinburgh: T&T Clark, 1995) 119–225

Hengel, M., 'The Song about Christ in Earliest Worship', *Studies in Early Christology* 227–91

Hengel, M., *Studien zur Christologie: Kleine Schriften IV* (WUNT 201; Tübingen: Mohr Siebeck, 2006)

Horbury, W., 'The Cult of Christ and the Cult of the Saints', *NTS* 44 (1998) 444–69

Horbury, W., 'Jewish and Christian Monotheism in the Herodian Age', in L. T. Stuckenbruck and W. E. S. North (eds), *Early Jewish and Christian Monotheism* 16–44

Horbury, W., *Jewish Messianism and the Cult of Christ* (London: SCM Press, 1998)

Hossfeld, F. L., and Kindl, E.-M., "*qārā*", in Botterweck and Ringgren (eds), *Theological Dictionary of the Old Testament* (ET; Grand Rapids: Eerdmans, 1974–2006) 13.113–15

Hurtado, L. W., *At the Origins of Christian Worship: The Context and Character of Earliest Christian Devotion* (Grand Rapids: Eerdmans, 1999)

Hurtado, L. W., 'Early Jewish Opposition to Jesus-Devotion', *JTS* 50 (1999) 35–58

Hurtado, L. W., 'First Century Jewish Monotheism', *JSNT* 71 (1998) 3–26

Hurtado, L. W., *How on Earth Did Jesus Become a God? Historical Questions about Earliest Devotion to Jesus* (Grand Rapids: Eerdmans, 2005)

Hurtado, L. W., *Lord Jesus Christ: Devotion to Jesus in Earliest Christianity* (Grand Rapids: Eerdmans, 2003)

Hurtado, L. W., *One God, One Lord: Early Christian Devotion and Ancient Jewish Monotheism* (Philadelphia: Fortress, 1988)

Hurtado, L. W., 'Religious Experience and Religious Innovation in the New Testament', *JR* 80 (2000) 183–205

Jeremias, J., *The Prayers of Jesus* (London: SCM Press, 1967)

Jeremias, J., *New Testament Theology, Vol. 1: The Proclamation of Jesus* (London: SCM Press, 1971)

Jungmann, J. A., *The Place of Christ in Liturgical Prayer* (London: Chapman, 1965)

Kelly, J. N. D., *Early Christian Doctrine* (London: A. & C. Black, ²1960)

Kittel, G. and Friedrich, G. (eds), *Theological Dictionary of the New Testament* (ET; Grand Rapids: Eerdmans, 1964–76)

Kreitzer, L. J., *Jesus and God in Paul's Eschatology* (JSNTS 19; Sheffield: JSOT, 1987)

Kupp, D., *Matthew's Emmanuel: Divine Presence and God's People in the First Gospel* (SNTSMS 90; Cambridge: Cambridge University Press, 1996)

Lampe, G. W. H., *God as Spirit* (Oxford: Oxford University Press, 1977)

Landmesser, C., Eckstein, H.-J., Lichtenberger, H., *Jesus Christus als die Mitte der Schrift*; Otfried Hofius FS; BZNW 86 (Berlin: de Gruyter, 1997)

Levine, B. A., 'Scripture's Account: Idolatry and Paganism', in J. Neusner, et al., *Torah Revealed, Torah Fulfilled: Scriptural Laws in Formative Judaism and Earliest Christianity* (New York: T&T Clark, 2008)

Levison, J. R., *The Spirit in First Century Judaism* (Leiden: Brill, 1997)

McGrath, J. F., *The Only True God: Early Christian Monotheism in its Jewish Context* (Champaign: University of Illinois Press, 2009)

Mach, M., 'Concepts of Jewish Monotheism during the Hellenistic Period', in C. C. Newman, et al. (eds), *The Jewish Roots of Christological Monotheism* 21–42

McHugh, J. F., *John 1–4* (ICC; London: T&T Clark, 2009)

Moberly, R. W. L., 'How Appropriate is "Monotheism" as a Category for Biblical Interpretation?', in L. T. Stuckenbruck and W. E. S. North (eds), *Early Jewish and Christian Monotheism* 227–30

Moberly, R. W. L., 'Towards an Interpretation of the Shema', in C. Seitz and K. Greene-McCreight (eds), *Theological Exegesis: Essays in Honor of Brevard S. Childs* (Grand Rapids: Eerdmans, 1999) 124–44

Moulton, J. H. and Turner, N., *A Grammar of New Testament Greek*, Vol. III (Edinburgh: T&T Clark, 1963)

Neusner, J., Chilton, B., and Levine, B. A., *Torah Revealed, Torah Fulfilled: Scriptural Laws in Formative Judaism and Earliest Christianity* (New York: T&T Clark, 2008)

Newman, C. C., Davila, J. A., and Lewis, G. S. (eds), *The Jewish Roots of Christological Monotheism* (JSJSupp 63; Leiden: Brill, 1999)

North, J. L., 'Jesus and Worship, God and Sacrifice', in L. T. Stuckenbruck and W. E. S. North (eds), *Early Jewish and Christian Monotheism* 186–202

Rahner, K., *The Trinity* (London: Burns & Oates, 1970)

Rainbow, P., 'Jewish Monotheism as the Matrix for New Testament Christology: A Review Article', *NovT* 33 (1991) 78–91

Richardson, N., *Paul's Language about God* (JSNTS 99; Sheffield Academic Press, 1993)

Rowland, C., *The Open Heaven: A Study in Apocalyptic Judaism and Early Christianity* (London: SPCK, 1982)

Sanders, E. P., *Jesus and Judaism* (London: SCM Press, 1985)

Sanders, E. P., *Judaism: Practice and Belief 63 BCE – 66 CE* (London: SCM Press, 1992)

Sawyer, J. F. A., 'Biblical Alternatives to Monotheism', *Theology* 87 (1984) 172–80

Schmidt, K. L., article in G. Kittel and G. Friedrich (eds), *Theological Dictionary of the New Testament* (ET; Grand Rapids: Eerdmans, 1964–76) 3.499–500

Schrage, W., *Der erste Brief an die Korinther* (EKK VII/2; Zurich: Benziger, 1995)

Schürer, E., *The History of the Jewish People in the Age of Jesus Christ* (ed. G. Vermes, et al., 4 vols; Edinburgh: T&T Clark, 1973–87)

Segal, A., 'Paul's "*SOMA PNEUMATIKON*" and the Worship of Jesus', in C. C. Newman, et al. (eds), *The Jewish Roots of Christological Monotheism* (*JSJ*Supp 63; Leiden: Brill, 1999) 258–76

Segal, A. F., *Two Powers in Heaven: Early Rabbinic Reports about Christianity and Gnosticism* (Leiden: Brill, 1977)

Seitz, C. and Greene-McCreight, K. (eds), *Theological Exegesis: Essays in Honor of Brevard S. Childs* (Grand Rapids: Eerdmans, 1999)

Smail, T. A., *The Forgotten Father* (London: Hodder & Stoughton, 1980)

Stuckenbruck, L. T., *Angel Veneration and Christology* (WUNT 2.70; Tübingen: Mohr Siebeck, 1995)

Stuckenbruck, L. T., '"Angels" and "God": Exploring the Limits of Early Jewish Monotheism', in L. T. Stuckenbruck and W. E. S. North (eds), *Early Jewish and Christian Monotheism* 45–70

Stuckenbruck, L. T., 'Worship and Monotheism in the *Ascension of Isaiah*', in C. C. Newman, et al. (eds), *The Jewish Roots of Christological Monotheism* 70–89

Stuckenbruck, L. T., and North, W. E. S. (eds), *Early Jewish and Christian Monotheism* (JSNTS 263; London: T&T Clark, 2004)

Thiselton, A. C., *The First Epistle to the Corinthians* (NIGTC; Grand Rapids: Eerdmans, 2000)

Thüsing, W., *Per Christum in Deum* (Münster: Aschendorff, 1965)

Urbach, E. E., 'Self-Isolation or Self-Affirmation in Judaism in the First Three Centuries: Theory and Practice', in E. P. Sanders (ed.),

Jewish and Christian Self-Definition: Vol. Two. Aspects of Judaism in the Graeco-Roman Period (London: SCM Press, 1981) 269–98

Vermes, G., *The Complete Dead Sea Scrolls in English* (London: Allen Lane/Penguin, 1997)

Whybray, R. N., *Wisdom in Proverbs* (London: SCM Press, 1965)

Witherington, B., *Jesus the Sage: The Pilgrimage of Wisdom* (Edinburgh: T&T Clark, 1994)

Wright, N. T., *The Climax of the Covenant* (Edinburgh: T&T Clark, 1991)

Index of biblical and ancient sources

Index of biblical and ancient sources

Index of biblical and ancient sources

162

Index of biblical and ancient sources

Index of modern authors

Index of subjects

Adam 88, 137; Adam
  Christology 127, 137–40,
  144–5, 148
angels 60–1, 66–71, 90, 92;
  of the presence 68, 71, 90;
  theophanic 67–8, 149;
  worship of 70–2, 90, 131
apotheosis 61, 84–9, 90
archangels 68–9

benediction 25–7

call upon the name of 15–16,
  18, 28
Christ: being in Christ 47,
  57; Christ-devotion 3, 29,
  113–16; divine/human 137,
  143; glory of 23–4, 28,
  119, 122; as High
  Priest 140–1; image of
  God 138, 147–8; as
  intercessor 140–1, 144–5,
  148; made perfect 139; as
  mediator 139–40, 145,
  148; pre-existence of 119;
  through Christ 21–2, 28, 57
christology 115–16;
  apocalyptic 131–2;
  functional 112, 141, 143;
  Modalism/
  Monarchianism 142;
  see also Logos christology,
  Spirit christology, Wisdom
  christology
divine agency 60, 105, 109,
  119, 142–5
divine hypostases 60–1, 76
divine identity 61, 79, 92–3,
  103, 107–10, 141–4
divine presence 46, 52, 57,
  59, 61, 67–73, 90–1, 123–4,
  126, 128–9, 132–4, 146,
  151
doxology 22–5, 133

early Christian experience
  102
Elijah 86–7, 102
emperor worship 103
Enoch 87–9, 102

God 6, 59; all in all 111–12,
  144, 151; Creator 143–4;
  crucified 150; Elohim 63;
  Father 27; glory of 24, 28,
  133; immanence of 60, 68,
  73–4, 90, 92, 93, 117, 120,

125–6, 143, 149, 151; of
  Israel 63, 65; a Jewish
  binitarianism? 74, 126; of
  the Lord Jesus Christ 3,
  110, 130, 136, 144–5;
  sovereign Ruler 144;
  un-image-(in)able 68, 73;
  unseeable 73, 121; vision
  of 69–70, 85; see also
  God-worshippers, grace
God-worshippers/fearers 17
grace 26–7; of the Lord Jesus
  Christ 26–7

heavenly intermediaries 60–1,
  79, 83, 142
henotheism 62
hymns 38–43; to Christ 38,
  42–3, 91; in praise of
  Christ 41–2, 57; psalms
  addressed to Christ 38–9

incarnation 120–2, 124–6

Jesus: authority of 99–100;
  a devout Jew 94–5, 101;
  as God 92, 115, 122, 130,
  132–6, 45; God's Son
  98–9, 101, 120–3, 136,
  139; as Lord 101–12,
  138–9, 145–6, 148; as
  Messiah 115–16, 145; a
  monotheist? 92, 93–101,
  145; praying 31, 37, 94–5,
  101, 144–5; resurrection
  of 101–2, 145; and the
  Shema 95–8; Son of
  man 100, 130, 132; through
  Jesus 21–2, 28, 59, 91, 101,
  107, 109–10, 122, 145–6,
  148, 150–1; Yahweh texts
  referred to 104–7; see also
  Jewish objections
Jesus-olatry 147–8
Jewish objections to Jesus as
  God 115

Logos christology 117–23,
  126, 134–6, 143, 145–6
Logos of God see Word
Lord as Jesus or God? 14,
  104–7
Lord's day 49
Lord's Prayer 97
Lord's Supper 50–1, 57

Melchizedek 88
Metatron 87–8

monolatry 62, 64
monotheism 60, 62–6, 84, 90,
  92, 107–9, 139–40;
  Christian monotheism 146,
  148–9, 151; Christological
  monotheism 4–5, 106–9;
  exclusive/inclusive 64
Moses, as god 66, 85–6

praise 19–20
prayer 15–16, 30–7; to
  God 33–4, 37; to
  Jesus 34–7, 57, 91; in the
  name of Jesus 33, 37, 91,
  145, 148; through Jesus
  Christ 21–2, 28, 59, 91
priests 51–2, 57

Sabbath 48–9
sacrifice 52–7, 91; Jesus' death
  as 55–7; 'ultimate criterion
  of deity' 53, 56
Shema 60, 62, 65–6, 94, 96,
  108–9; split *Shema* 109
Son of Man 87, 100
Spirit 6, 60–1, 72–4, 90, 92,
  116–17, 125–9, 145, 149;
  of Christ 127, 146; not
  worshipped 74, 129;
  Paraclete 128–9, 140;
  worship of 149; see also
  Spirit christology
Spirit christology 126–9

Temple 43–7, 54; Christian
  attitude to 44–6
thanksgiving 20–2, 27–8
theōsis 89
Trinity 1, 112; Jewish and
  Muslim attitudes to 1, 148,
  150; three persons 1, 112,
  142
two powers heresy 88, 100

Wisdom christology 117,
  123–6, 136, 143, 145–6
Wisdom of God 60–1, 74–9,
  90, 92, 109–10, 123–4, 149;
  identification with Torah
  77–8, 121–2; no cult
  of Wisdom 78; as
  personification 76–7,
  124; see also Wisdom
  christology
Word/Logos of God 60–1,
  79–84, 90, 92, 110, 111,
  118, 124, 149;
  personification 120; in